Prai

By Kim Ode

With photos by John Danicic Jr.

And an introduction by Ron Robinson

Ex Machina Publishing Co.
Sioux Falls, South Dakota

Much of the text in this book is reprinted from columns and articles by Kim Ode appearing in the Sioux Falls *Argus Leader* and the *Star Tribune* in Minneapolis. Applicable copyright and permission notices are printed in conjunction with each story.

Published by EX MACHINA PUBLISHING CO., Box 448, Sioux Falls, SD 57101.

First Edition
First Printing

Cover photos by John Danicic Jr.

Library of Congress Cataloging-in-Publication Data

Ode, Kim, 1955-
Prairie beat.
Includes index.
1. Iowa---Social life and customs. 2. South Dakota --Social life and customs. 3. Minnesota--Social life and customs. I. Title.
F625.034 1987 977 87-22366
ISBN 0-944287-01-8
ISBN 0-944287-00-X (pbk.)

Dedication:

To the people within whose stories are a continuing history of the prairie.

Acknowledgements

The author acknowledges with gratitude the encouragement she received from Larry Fuller, president and publisher of the Sioux Falls *Argus Leader*, under whose guidance many of these stories were written.

The author thanks her parents for getting used to reading about themselves every once in a while.

The publishers acknowledge the help they received in putting together this collection. The following people and institutions are prominent among the many who rendered invaluable aid:

Augustana College, Sioux Falls, S.D.
Lloyd Cunningham, photo editor, Sioux Falls *Argus Leader*.
John Danicic Jr., photographer, Minneapolis, Minn.
Jeff Danz, Lakeside Dairy, Sioux Falls, S.D.
Larry Fuller, president and publisher, Sioux Falls *Argus Leader*.
Bonnie Gardner, archivist, Robinson State Museum, Pierre, S.D.
Glenn Gering, Pine Hill Printery, Freeman, S.D.
John Hanners, Phd., Allegheny College, Meadeville, Penn.
David B. Hartley, director, Robinson State Museum, Pierre, S.D.
Bill Hoskins, Old Courthouse Museum, Sioux Falls, S.D.
Carol Mashek, president, Minnehaha Historical Society, Sioux Falls, S.D.
Terrie Miesen, Tri-State Graphics, Sioux Falls, S.D.
Jim Osberg, Robinson State Museum, Pierre, S.D.
John Rychtarik, curator, Old Court House Museum, Sioux Falls, S.D.
Hal Seymour, *Star Tribune*, Minneapolis, Minn.
Joseph Stuart, Memorial Art Museum, Brookings, S.D.
Harry Thompson, archivist, Center for Western Studies, Augustana College, Sioux Falls, S.D.
Leonard Tripp, vice president, Minnehaha Historical Society, Sioux Falls, S.D.

Introduction: On being a writer

"I think I've found what I want to do with my life."

The woman standing in the doorway of my office delivered the sentence with a shy firmness with which I had become familiar over two years. Here was a person at once deferential and confident. And when she said something with that tone, she left do doubt that she meant it. So I had good reason to quake at the words: I was witnessing someone in the midst of making a life-shaping decision, the choice of a vocation. After a short experience as an intern, Kim Ode had concluded that she wanted to be a reporter.

I had no doubt that she could write well; she had proven that in class assignments. But writing is only part of being a reporter. The rest of it has to do with aggressiveness, tough skin, skepticism, and an indefatigable curiosity. My sense at the time was that she would be sadly out of place among the cynics and go-getters of the press. Besides, it is always disconcerting to hear a young person declare enthusiastically for any career without knowing what he or she is getting into. How often have parental and professorial insides sunk in response to such affirmations: "I want to be an actor." "I want to be a lawyer." "I want to be a writer."

(I am reminded of the three pieces of advice offered recently by a friend of mine — an experienced publisher — in response to my suggestion that publishing might be a good line to pursue: "One — Don't do it. Two — Don't do it. Three — Don't do it.")

However, I fought my instincts and did not discourage Kim Ode from becoming a reporter. And sure enough, time has shown my instincts in this case to be mistaken. Within a few years she had became one of the most popular columnists ever to write for the Sioux Falls *Argus Leader*. Later she stood herself in good stead as a feature writer for the Rochester, N.Y., *Times-*

Union before returning to the Midwest to write for the *Minneapolis Star and Tribune.* After a decade as a successful-newspaper writer, she is safe in feeling that her vocational-choice was a good one. Nevertheless, I am still struck by differences between her demeanor and that of many tooth-and-nail reporters. It is these attributes that make her a superb columnist and feature writer: a love for common people, a respect for tradition, a strong sense of place, an attention to colorful detail, an awe for the slow turning of time.

Prairie Beat contains abundant evidence of each of these attributes.

Granted that some of the people Kim writes about here are truly extraordinary (Richard Cropp and Ralph Cook come to mind), a reader gets the impression that all people are seen by this writer as special in one way or another. Arthur Miller's plea on behalf of Willy Loman — "Attention must be paid to this man!" — seems to have been taken seriously and applied broadly by Kim Ode. The wisecracking fruitseller, the garbage-hauling widow, the self-made inventor, the rodeo cowboy, the unassuming grandmother — all loom as large and as important in her writing as any celebrity. Perhaps only one who has been raised on a farm or in a small town where individual characteristics are closely noted could write so appealingly of such men and women. There is none of the leveling stare of the city in these pieces, no cynical assumption about "the masses." While a common humanity is discerned, uncommon traits are highlighted with the skill of a sculptor or a portrait painter. What is felt in these profiles goes beyond sympathy. It approaches the empathy stirred by great art.

Still more rare in this era of pop-music aesthetics is Kim Ode's respect for the rituals and ceremonies that have sustained communities and societies over decades or even centuries. Ludefisk dinners, meat-packing socials, Sunday drives, and ice-harvest revivals are all appropriate and affecting subjects for this writer. What she emphasizes in them is neither the quaintness nor the incongruity of such events, but rather the comforting effect of tradition. Individual human beings die, but traditions go on. Even when activities such as making rhubarb wine are driven to the verge of extinction by technology and pre-packaged, mass-manufactured "convenience," they are recognized as worthy of continuation on the grounds that they provide a sense of shared humanity and of hope. You can't lay up meat for the winter or bottle wine that has to age for a year if you believe that the world will end tomorrow. These pages are filled with people doing things that they seem to enjoy doing as much for the repeated pleasure of the company of co-workers and for the repeated pleasure of the work intself as for the pay. "No one wants to do this dirty job," a sheep shearer says. But he's done it for decades to the accompaniment of banter with his partner. "You get the dumb stuff in your blood," a stonecutter explains. A reader comes to suspect that Kim Ode would justify her work in similar terms.

Teachers of writing sometimes warn students of the danger of becoming too closely assocated with a particular locale or region. Nearly forgotten writers such as Zona Gale or George Washington Cable are cited as examples of such parochialism. Writers like William Faulkner or Sinclair Lewis or Flannery O'Connor are conveniently ignored in this argument. The truth may be that all notable writers are conscious of place and that they differ only in the size of the turf that they cut out for themselves. Ernest Hemingway's Spain or Cuba or Italy or Africa seem as uniquely his literary landscape as Yoknapatawpha is Faulkner's. Ironically, the same teachers who warn writers about regionalism are often those who hold as a treasured dictum "Write about what you know best." Perhaps they are not aware of Henry James' classic rejoinder: "Be one upon whom nothing is lost." All of the foregoing is not to suggest that Kim Ode is another Flannery O'Connor, or even that she is another Zona Gale. Rather, it is to defend her obvious affinity for the Midwest in this collection. She was born and raised near the juncture of South Dakota, Minnesota, and Iowa; and most of her subject matter is drawn from this tri-state region. She knows the place well and she writes about it with beauty and passion. Here is the way she begins one story: "The walls of the trench are sharp with broken buffalo bones. Heat rises in shimmers from the crisp grass, blurring a distant grove of trees and intensifying the keen smell of creosote from the old railroad ties that mark a path through the rolling acre." Who else would think to start a piece about archeology this way? Who else could evoke pipestone quarries, abandoned cemeteries, or lichen-covered rock outcroppings as clearly as someone who finds herself completely at home in these surroundings? Who else would find them worth evoking? Even for those who have not shared these landscapes, Kim Ode's descriptions must provide that shock or recognition which is the mark of effective writing.

You cannot read far in Kim Ode's work without realizing that she knows the names of things: trees, flowers, birds, cheeses. There is a specificity in her writing that is reminiscent of the journals of Dorothy Wordsworth, whose notations were the source of many of the best poems of her brother William — although Dorothy's writing was less cosmic. This ability to tell the difference between an elm and a hackberry is especially-impressive to those of us who grew up surrounded by a-variety of plants and animals that we could identify only in the broadest generic terms. Yet the least knowledgeable of us could hardly fail to recognize the poetry and precision of such exact citations. When naming is augmented by equally poetic and precise description, a reader is drawn into a magical world in which imagination is used not to create unicorns and dragons, but to allow us to see the reality around us as though we were experiencing it for the first time: "There is something about light at dusk, even if the sky is draped over the land like a damp gray blanket. A red barn and a white house reflect the pale glow of an invisible sun as day passes imperceptibly into evening. A farmplace floats in a sea as green as dollar bills." And when Kim Ode describes a scene out of her memory, we feel as though we are somehow remembering it ourselves: "Summers were wonderful in that grove. The trees grew in those familiar, even rows that distinguish a prairie tamed. On the outside were Russian olives, then some cottonwoods, then maybe five rows of ash. Each pair of rows created long alleys paved with grass."

The greatest difference between Kim Ode and many of her contemporary reporters, however, is that she is aware of time on a larger and slower scale. It is easy for a newswriter — beset by deadlines and constantly reminded of what is current and what is old news — to get lost in the superficial flow of events and to break contact with the rhythms of the seasons, the ebb and flow of the years and of the centuries. But in *Prairie Beat* there is heard the even drumming of the passing ages. While this painful awareness of time and change leads to nostalgia that seems odd in one so young, it is the source as well of a healing resignation. Speaking of a 300-year-old bur oak, she summons the eons: "It was a sapling when Johann Sebastian Bach was in diapers, 60 years old by the time the first French explorers ventured into the Dakotas. Settlers hunted with their new repeating rifles beneath the boughs of the 180-year-old tree. Thirty years later, they might have gathered under its wintry branches to piece together rumors of a massacre of Indians at Wounded Knee." And after remarking that the tree is probably in its last seasons, she adds, "Then again, that's probably what some old fur trapper thought." She takes a similar long view with the Blue Mound in Minnesota and with an old stage stop in South Dakota. An imagination that can transcend time in this way must provide a consolation of the highest order: a sense of the continuity of the universe in the midst of the flickering images of life and change.

There is much that I see I have left out of this catalog of virtues: a gentle humor, a thirst for the details of history, a penchant for a good yarn. But if I were to go on much further, I might stretch the credulity of the reader. Kim Ode is a remarkable writer, I believe, but I do not want to suggest that she is supernatural. It is enough to say that she is one of those fortunate few who have found occupations that best match their talents

Read on and discover for yourself.

Ron Robinson

Preface:
On going away

Jake Voight was on his umpteenth card trick and I was on my umpteenth cup of coffee.

The question was how to best end this interview for, of course, it was time to leave Wall Lake and get back to work. Deadlines, you know.

"Hey," Jake said, perhaps sensing my restlessness, "what have we got but time?"

And I learned another card trick.

Don't ask me to repeat the trick; I forget things like that as quickly as a cat forgets a kindness. But I remember Jake's words, especially on those frantic days when it seems the minute hand sweeps away time like rain from a windshield.

There is a lot to be learned from the people I've met through my job. By and large, they are people with basic truths to be shared, good wishes to be conveyed. They do not change the course of humanity; they are the course humanity takes.

That is why I'm choosing to reflect upon them now with the sort of regurgitative ramblings that a final column requires. This is my last column for the Argus Leader; I've taken another job as a feature writer in Rochester, N.Y., but I'll try to take some of the common sense I've learned here out there.

It's the sense, for instance, that comes from Harvey Woods, an old beer vendor at Metropolitan Stadium in Minneapolis who captured the hearts and thirsts of the folks in Delmont, S.D. Two summers ago, they adopted him for a week, showing him the kind of good time only a pig roast, Missouri swim and tour of the Corn Palace could bring.

"Living right, eating right and treating people right — you have to keep this feeling about you," he said when we visited.

It's the sense that comes from Ralph Cook, a biology teacher from Brandon, S.D., who retired last spring after 35 years in the classroom.

"When you get out of the hole yourself, it helps you understand these students," he said. "You love them more. It's better than if you had the glory road all the way."

It's even the sense voiced by Gert Bidne who, at 83, still is proprietress of Bidne's Dress and Shoe Shop in Flandreau, S.D,

"You get some women in their 60s who come in and carry on and carry on like it was their last day on earth," she said. "When I get to feeling what I call unnecessary, I just peel my clothes and crawl into bed. The next morning, everything's roses."

The point of this, I guess, is that we must respect ourselves and know our pace. We needn't rush through life, but neither should we allow ourselves to be lulled by complacency. These people, however content they appear to be, have not let contentment stifle their need to lead vital lives.

Perhaps it is a fear of complacency — of contentment too easily gained — that is leading me away, at least for a while. I am comfortable here. I do not expect to feel as secure for some time, yet I am excited by the challenge of regaining it.

I'm not sure why I feel the need to explain my actions, though it's probably rooted in my defensive attitude toward South Dakota. In other words, I want to say that I'm not leaving because this is a hick state and I'm after the big time. I'm leaving because I have to know what it's like to leave a place you love.

There is another world out there to explore — a world with trees, as one of my colleagues says. Who knows? I may be back. It's happened to countless other Midwesterners.

After all, there are challenges to living right here, no matter how solid things seem. Maybe the greatest challenge is finding challenges where there appear to be few.

Jake Voight, Ralph Cook and Gert Bidne have found this to be so. Now it's my turn.

— and on coming home

Oh, such serious thoughts. It was a big deal, leaving home, but I'm back now. Always figured I would be, which sometimes makes me wonder if I ever gave New York a fair shake. Other times, I know it was inevitable. I am a product of this environment, with its wide horizons, coffee black and weather that revels in extremes.

I have to say, though, that it was good to go away. The reasons change as often as a stoplight, but they come together in all sorts of ways to affect how I think about things.

But it's good to be back among the people like those I visited with over the years, better to meet more of them, best to feel as though I'm one of them. Besides, no one in New York appreciated ludefisk jokes.

August 1987
Kim Ode

Contents

"Who..."

"What..."

"Where..."

WINTER

"When..."

The fine art of keeping warm

We know what winter can do to a person. Valley Forge, the high school tournament blizzards — history is littered with the havoc this season has wrought. Tomorrow, it returns.

Optimists say tomorrow is the shortest day of the year, that the sun will start shining longer soon. Be forewarned. This is mere meteorological subterfuge to divert us from the challenge faced by humanity ever since the first lake froze over: keeping warm. It has taken its toll.

Consider how many women, who were youngsters in the days before school dress codes allowed jeans and before leggings were stylish, still suffer the mortifying effects of having had to wear slacks under their skirts. It was bad enough that you looked like one of those dancing hippos in *Fantasia*, but you had to develop a knack for swiftly pulling them on and off among the furtive glances of the boys in the coat room.

Or consider the numbers of men who each winter are compelled to let their faces get hairy because they think it's sissy to wear a muffler and hat and figure their own home-grown afghan will keep them warm. Worse, a beard carries all those connotations of masculinity so the sensibly dressed, clean-shaven man feels doubly snowballed.

Or consider the children gathered on street corners on week-day mornings. True, they look bright as hard candy in their nylon and Gore-Tex. Yet their profiles remain determinedly bulky with scarves wound twice around their necks while Moon boots make their calves resemble Popeye's forearms. And science still hasn't figured how to make children's bladders shut down once their snowsuits go on.

It's not easy, yet we endure.

One reason is put forth is a book called *Comfort Below Freezing* by Robert McQuilken. It's all about winter camping, but between chapters on ski wax and physical conditioning, he tells why human beings don't make like bears and find a cave.

"Humans," he writes, "unlike other species, have the power to adapt (cognitively). If their environment is unsatisfactory, they are able to recognize this and create the means for changing it through the use of tools."

This does not mean using the instant cash machine to withdraw plane fare for Jamaica. A tool in this case can be a sweater or an igloo. Or a mug of Tom 'n Jerry.

McQuilken offers some practical tips for keeping warm. Wool is best — for underwear, for socks, for your head. You're not supposed to dress so heavily that you sweat, but if you do, wool wicks it away from your body better than cotton. Speaking of your head, keep it covered. Your parents may have told you your body is a temple, but it's a temple with a flue.

When you get cold from standing around, do isometrics. Tense your whole body for 15 seconds, then relax. Repeating this should warm you. Shivering, by the way, is the body's involuntary form of isometrics.

Then there's the handy-dandy car emergency kit: a candle in a coffee can, (light the candle and the warmed can will radiate heat), a half-dozen candy bars and a blanket. All this practicality is well and good, but surely there are more creative means of maintaining a healthy 98.6 degrees. These theories have not received much publicity, but we'll throw them out, along with some salt for the sidewalk.

•The theory of visual warmth. Clearly, possession of a fireplace is nine-tenths of the thaw, but not everyone is so fortunate. Lacking a hearth, assemble your own with a display of massed candles. (Even better, save your empty waxed milk cartons over the next week and have a candle-making extravaganza.)

•The theory of borrowed warmth. Romance notwithstanding, you can't cuddle all evening and still get the Sinatra biography read. Adopt a cat. Living pelts, they spread across your lap, only too willing to share their body heat. Purring, while not proven to be warm in and of itself, doesn't hurt.

•The theory of liquid warmth. Steeping some gingerroot in a small pot of boiling water then adding it to the tub is supposed to make you feel all warm and tingly. Or simply use enough bubble bath (more, just a little more) to trap the water's heat beneath the froth, the better to keep your knees warm.

•The theory of imagined warmth. Another library book, *Winter Activities* by Molly Redmond, tells how to force a branch into early bloom. The first step is careful thawing, in cold water first, then warm if you picked it in below-freezing weather. Then place it in a bucket of water in a cool room with indirect light. Once the flower buds swell, you can bring it into a slightly warmer room. Good branches include pussy willows, red maples, forsythia, wild plum and birch.

As a last resort, you can revel in the cold. Both Redmond and McQuilken recount the joys of homemade ice cream made by simply pouring sweetened condensed milk (not evaporated milk) over a bowl of snow. Throw in some frozen blue-berries and you have a dessert fit for a k-k-k-king. Or q-q-queen.

The year came in — with a bang!

"'I knew what I'd get and I got it,'she said, lying on a snow-white hospital bed, occasionally lifting her head to look about, a bandage over one eye where the bullet struck."

So began Helen Seiler's tale of sex and violence, death and dynamite, mobsters and murder that literally rocked Sioux Falls on New Year's Eve 44 years ago tonight and made the city the center of national attention.

Almost anyone who lived here in the 1930s already knows what this is about. Few fail to muster a memory of the man blown to smithereens, the woman who miraculously escaped death and the concussion that broke windows 30 miles away in Dell Rapids in what has come to be known as The Powderhouse Blast.

The New Year's Day headlines fairly screamed:

"Three Hunted For Death Blast, Wounding of Girl in Gang Row."

"Mobsters eliminate Companion by Blowing Him to Pieces."

Sure beats the socks off reading about the unemployment rate and Nancy's plans for redecorating the White House. Not that anyone wants to go back to those days of cement shoes and long rides, of course, but it makes for a good yarn.

Just ask Seldon Lacey. He was one of those who found Helen Seiler in a ditch, eight bullets piercing her 25-year-old body and half of her coat blown away by the blast.

"Yeah, that was quite a thing," Lacey said recently from his home in rural Valley Springs. "I thought I heard somebody call for help, but then a lot of people were showing up and I wasn't sure.

"We walked away from the crowd and I said, 'Let's go home the north way,' and there she was, lying in the ditch.

"It was quite a deal."

The episode began with the robbery of $37,000 from a Sioux City jewelry store. The gang of four men and Mrs. Seiler fled

90 miles north to Sioux Falls where she and her sweetheart, Harold Baker, decided to turn themselves in to the authorities.

The other members of the gang got wind of their plan and, "to prevent them from 'squawking,'" took the couple five miles southeast of Sioux Falls to the Larson Hardware Co. powderhouse under the pretense of burglarizing it.

Once there, they slugged Mrs. Seiler with a hammer, then shot her. Baker also was knocked out and both were dragged into the powderhouse where they lay slumped among 7,500 pounds of powder and 3,000 pounds of dynamite. Before the gangsters left, seven more bullets were fired into her body.

The fuse was lit.

Mrs Seiler, known as "a habitue of the Sioux City red light district," had been with the gang only three weeks. She'd left her alcoholic husband — who later was to say that he "still loved her" — and took up with Baker, a paroled convict from California.

"Gee he was swell," she said from her hospital bed when asked about the dead man. "I met him when I was drunk."

Lee Bradley, a South Dakota bank robber, William Nesbeth, a Sioux City bartender, and Harry "Slim" Reeves, a Sioux City desperado, were the guts of the gang. They had just blown a safe at Ehlermann Wholesale Jewelry in Sioux City and came to Sioux Falls for another robbery.

They were not murderers, yet murder became a necessity.

Lacey, who lived less than a mile from the powderhouse, saw the flash light up the evening sky. He, Ed Lacey and John Rohl drove to the site, thinking that someone shooting rabbits had mistakenly shot into the concrete block house.

In downtown Sioux Falls, New Year's Eve revelers thought a bomb had been dropped, that a meteor had exploded, or that a locomotive had blown up. People poured out of bars and restaurants into the streets to see the imagined destruction.

It wasn't all imagined: More than $20,000 worth of windows were broken in the city, as well as windows in Dell Rapids, 30 miles to the north. Residents of Pipestone, Minn., felt the concussion, as did people in Doon, Iowa.

Arriving on the scene, Lacey saw a huge crater that later was measured to be 24x35 feet across and 25 feet deep. The powderhouse was reduced to some concrete fragments lying in a jumble. The snow for hundreds of yards around was melted.

Mrs. Seiler, who had dragged herself out of the house when she saw the sizzling fuse, was found in a ditch about 200 feet from the site, bloodied and incoherent with one leg frozen from exposure.

Only after she had been treated for severe shock and regained her senses did police learn that Harold Baker had been in that powderhouse.

Later that evening, "a piece of flesh was brought to police headquarters by J.W. Higgins, a Sioux Falls salesman. It was turned over to a physician for examination. Higgins found it about 200 feet east of the powderhouse. It was believed to be a piece of Baker's shattered body."

Tests revealed that it was.

A manhunt — "one of the most intense and farflung the northwest has ever seen" — began for the three men with "Slim" Reeves being captured three days later in a farmer's garage near Sioux City. By the time the next sun set, he'd been sentenced to 40 years in the Iowa State Prison for the jewelry store robbery and faced a South Dakota murder charge upon his release.

As Lacey remembers, all the gang members eventually were captured. Mrs. Seiler survived, but her eventual fate is uncertain. Some say she traveled with a circus sideshow for some time. Others say she married a farmer in Minnesota.

No one knows whether she is alive today.

Originally published 12-31-80 as "S.F. blast still intriguing tale 44 years later."

Glass bottles and cream-topped milk

With regret, Chris Christopherson remembers when the cream he delivered was so thick, you could hardly pour it from the carton.

With fondness, he remembers when milk wasn't homogenized, allowing the customer the pleasure of swirling the layer of cream deep into the glass bottle.

With consternation, he remembers the day they replaced Dan with a truck.

Christopherson delivered milk in Sioux Falls for 30-some years, about half that time with Dan, a bull of a horse who followed Christopherson up the block as he made his daily dairy delivery.

"When I got the truck, I was so mad," he says. "They wouldn't keep running like a horse could. With a truck, you didn't say 'whoa,' you just pushed on the gas."

What might simply have been called Christopherson's memories took on the significance of history when Terrace Park Dairy last Friday discontinued home delivery.

The end was inevitable, general manager James D. Jensen says.

In fact, Sioux Falls was one of the last bastions of doorstep dairying in metropolitan areas. Increases in the number of grocery stores, the cost of repairs and the price of fuel combined to scuttle Terrace Park's five routes remaining in the city. The price difference between home-delivered and store-bought milk also continued to widen, from $2.21 for a delivered gallon of low-fat milk to as low as $1.59 a gallon in the grocery cooler.

Women's liberation also played an important role in the demise since few homes are occupied during the day.

"It's pretty tough to deliver a perishable product when more than 60 percent of the women here are working," Jensen says.

"We had trouble with hours, whether to get them before 8 o'clock or after 5."

Christopherson never would have had that trouble, partly because he worked when times were different and trust was more freely given.

He began delivering milk for Lakeside Dairy in 1939, hitching up Dan seven days a week to plod over a route from 10th Street to Grange Avenue and from 18th Street to Eighth Street, about 80-100 customers in all.

In the summer, he piled ice in the wagon; in winter, he stoked the charcoal stove to keep the milk from freezing.

"I just know damn well — excuse me — that we just delivered quarts, pints and half-pints back then," he says, straining to retrieve a shred of memory. "There were no gallons."

He'd complete his daily route by 10 or 11 a.m. — after a couple of kitchen-table coffee breaks — "then we'd have a beer and play a lot of ball."

On a milk route around 1930. Chris Christopherson got started with Lakeside Dairy in 1939: "When I got the truck I was so mad. They wouldn't keep running like a horse could." (Photo courtesy Lakeside Dairy.)

Christopherson was not just a milkman.

"Oh, I had a pocketful of keys so I could let myself in, put it in the refrigerator. I was a good alarm clock, too, since I was never off more than five minutes, so sometimes I had to wake 'em up.

"Then there were some places I had to let the dog out and tie it up."

His rewards for such beyond-the-call-of-duty favors usually were full of calories or high in alcoholic content. There was one Christmas, though, that he recalls for the 17 ties he received.

"And they were those big jobs, you know," he says, his laugh lines becoming deep creases with the memory.

Christopherson joined Terrace Park in 1958 and retired six years ago, although he's still on the payroll working for public relations, going to the stores "and pushing that fruit drink, ice cream and cottage cheese."

At 67, he is a fortunate casualty of changing times. The five men who drove the last of their twice-a-week delivery routes on Friday have been laid off, victims of a convenience that became a luxury.

Although Terrace Park commissioned a scientific survey that spelled out the end, a fair number of gray hairs were produced in making the decision, Jensen says.

"When you've done something for 32 years, it's hard to just up and quit."

Today, Christopherson raises pheasants on his farm near Viborg. Dan has long since gone on to that great Milky Way in the sky. Paper cartons have replaced glass bottles ("the greatest thing that ever happened") and prices, well, prices have gone up.

There was a time, Christopherson says with a distant smile, that he delivered a quart of milk to the back porch for 14 cents.

UPDATE: In his retirement, Christopherson enjoys golfing, hunting, fishing, and working his farm.

Minnehaha Springs — on again, off again

They first gurgled with healing waters revered by the Sioux, then soaked the lolling masses waiting for their divorces to come through.

The Minnehaha Springs have been bottled and bubbled, capped and tapped. They've been harnessed for some years now, channeled into the plumbing of a nearby house, or simply stoppered, seeping beneath the surface of Cathedral Hill.

Well, it looks like the spring has sprung.

Not much; no gushers here. But the removal of a house to make way for an eventual school appears to have dislodged the cap on one of the several springs, sending a trickle across a vacant lot and east down Fourth Avenue.

It most likely will simply be recapped, yet it's exciting news for Carol Mashek, a local historian who has suspected a spring flowed beneath the house that once served as the YWCA, but never was able to prove it. She's researched the history of the springs, especially since plans were made to build a grade school atop the hill that she likens to a sponge, and spins quite a yarn about the now-trampled area that once sported one of the most beautiful parks in Sioux Falls.

Legend says the springs, called "Minne Waukon" or sacred water by the Sioux, were said to have medicinal purposes. Area tribes brought their sick to the waters that were marked by tying the branches of a young tree to the ground so that when it matured, all the limbs would grow down.

The pioneer movement soon claimed Sioux Falls for its own, however, and in 1881, the Heynsohn brothers, whose soda pop business on Phillips Avenue was wiped out by the great flood of that spring, bought the property and opened Minnehaha Bottling Works.

Business thrived during this period of epidemic disease, the pure spring water easing the fears of a city that drew its public water directly from the Big Sioux River. Some people, however,

Minnehaha Springs in full flow in the late 1800s. At the time it was known as Heynsohn Springs. The wooden foutain is now housed in the Old Courthouse Museum. (Photo courtesy Sioux-land Heritage Museums.)

---

preferred even more "medicinal" waters with the result that the brothers expanded in 1891, building the Keeley Institute to the south.

The Keeley Method was a 28-day treatment for alcohol and drug addiction, using what was known as The Gold Cure. The process involved a gradual withdrawal from alcohol with some tippling allowed each day in addition to drinking and bathing in the mineral water.

But such institutes needed alcoholics to survive and, with the advent of Prohibition in 1919, it went out of business.

In the meantime, C. Fred H. Witte had been hired as manager of the bottling works, adding a public bathing section to the business and overseeing the landscaping of the hillside behind their building.

The Minnehaha Springs baths became a hot spot for those who had come to get a quickie divorce under South Dakota's six months' residency, mainly because local hotels had few bathtubs.

The entire east side of the hill was landscaped with arbors and flower beds with a fountain sparkling in the middle. The park became a favorite spot for young ladies to promenade on Sunday afternoons.

That died after the 1908 Legislature, properly shocked at the record 145 divorces granted that year, raised residency requirements to one year.

In the meantime, Witte expanded the bottling business, then started manufacturing paint, the formula of which later was sold to become Sioux Falls Paint and Glass when the oils needed for the manufacture of paint became scarce during World War II.

Wartime sugar rationing also spelled the end of the bottling industry and the building was sold to Frank's Frozen Foods; in 1973, it was sold to Sioux Sound.

Today, there is little evidence that a park once graced the overgrown hillside. Some concrete mounds mark where the springs have been capped and there is a depression where the fountain stood. The fountain—made, surprisingly, of wood—is still around, owned by the Leon Watne family, but has fallen into disrepair.

It is into the Watne's home that the springs still run, ebbing during dry times and flowing when some rain falls. It's good water, Mrs. Watne says, "although I don't know if you'd call it curative. If you were lacking some minerals, then I suppose it would be good for you."

As usual, the legend makes a better story.

Originally published 2-11-81 as "Minnehaha Springs doing a slow flow again."

UPDATE: Hawthorne school now occupies the site of Minnehaha Springs.

"Who..."

Pick a card

Taking the pot from the living room heater — "Here, let me tune up your coffee" — Jake Voight settles in to tell yet another story about Wall Lake.

He's already talked about being pals with Lawrence Welk, gone through the history of the four Wall Lake Pavilions he and his father built and reminisced about the ice harvest.

He's explained his ancestry (High German) and marveled at the amount of open water on Wall Lake.

"This is the first time I saw it open up in February," he says in a voice as raw as a March breeze off the water. "That is something."

Voight is a trademark of Wall Lake, a barnacle of sorts that latched on in 1913 and, except for five miserable years in Minnesota, has stuck here ever since.

His real name is Orlow, but he's been Jake since he was 12. Once, he won an expensive gun under the name of Orlow Voight and no one could figure out who that was.

He's one of those people who came here long ago and, with a succession of odd jobs to support the rural roulette of farming, has lived a comfortable life. Retired now, he offers a wealth of chatting — don't call it history — about this place that's become a liquid oasis to landlocked Sioux Falls and is simply home to him and his wife, Alma.

"Yeah, I can remember coming here on a hayrack with my mom driving the team of horses," he says. They settled on the southeast end of the lake, where a barn with the legend, "Lake View Farm" still stands.

Within a couple of years, his father built a dance pavilion on his farm, a spot that sported the area's first pop stand as well as being a place for folks like Lawrence Welk and his Novelty Band to play.

("By gosh, he made himself famous, didn't he?")

As the crowds grew, the old pavilion came down and was replaced by a larger one, a process that went on until the fourth

Orlow "Jake" Voight at Wall Lake. "Yeah, I can remember coming here on a hayrack." (ARGUS LEADER photo by John Danicic Jr., reprinted by permission.)

and last one was built in 1936, down where the boat ramp is today.

"Yeah, we had an all-maple floor. Men got in for a dollar and women were free. And for that, they got coffee and cake. I believe we even gave a sandwich out, too. Our biggest crowd was 1,100 paid admissions."

The lake dried up in 1937, though, victim of the great drought that shriveled the nation, and with it went the prosperity of those Lindy Hopping days.

The lake came back, of course, gurgling to life from the many springs that trickle from the natural rock wall forming most of the shoreline. In time, Voight cut back on his farming and began selling lots.

"What I sold for $375, the guy's now getting $2,000," he says without a trace of bitterness. He still owns about 70 acres after giving a couple to one of his two sons when he married and remains a strong believer in the land ethic.

"Land—that, they can't take that away from you," he says, the lines around his lake-blue eyes deepening with the thought. Today, there is little open land around Wall Lake, with steady shoreline growth since the late 1950s. Some fear the lake is dying, but Voight's catches of perch, northern and a few walleye seem to belie that theory, although he figures there's six feet of mud on the bottom.

His view of the lake has changed, too, with the 3,000 or so trees he planted having grown up. That may change again soon, unfortunately, for most of them were elms, now ravaged by Dutch elm disease.

"Yeah, the elm, he was a good tree."

Still, it's obvious that Jake and Alma love their modest turquoise house decorated with family photos and old, satiny pillows touting the U.S. Army, a house in which he calls her "Momma" and she calls him "Angel." They're celebrating their 39th wedding anniversary today.

"No, I wouldn't live in that goddang California if they give me a free house," Angel, er, Voight says. "I'd rather live in the Badlands — and that might not be bad."

Looking forward to his 72nd birthday in July, he's starting to reminisce more these days, remembering the people who backed their buggies up to fish, thinking about the six drowned men he's pulled from the lake.

He talks about making an onion calendar — an old wives' tale that requires slicing a large onion into 12 pieces with each piece telling you what kind of weather to expect each month, depending on whether the slice is juicy or dry.

He recalls Lake City, a nonexistent place just across the field to the east where the local post office once stood.

Most of all, he recalls a card trick — or two or three.

"Hey," he says, deftly dealing to a visiting patsy, "what have we got but time?"

UPDATE: Jake Voight is still at Wall Lake, doing well.

The birder caged

OWATONNA, Minn. — It was Christmas Day. Terry Savaloja had to call his family from jail in Miami. And all for a glimpse of a spot-breasted oriole.

The tale goes something like this: Savaloja, one of the best birders in Minnesota, heard that the rare oriole was in a South Miami neighborhood. For two days, he ambled the Miami streets without luck, so he left to check out a report of a red-whiskered bulbo farther down the coast. He returned to Miami for one last exploration, but with no better luck.

"I was about ready to give up when the police swarmed in — pulled right up on the curb in back of me — and the detective comes up and says, 'Look, we can do this two ways: We can arrest you or you can come down to the station for questioning.'"

Turns out a resident of that neighborhood was robbed of $100,000 in jewels. Savaloja's meanderings suddenly were deemed mysterious by neighbors and the police were summoned. Fortunately, Savaloja keeps a diary of all his birding expeditions. It showed he was not in South Miami the day of the robbery. The woman whose hedge he had haunted for the red-whiskered bulbo corroborated his story.

He missed the oriole on that trip, but caught up with one later, he says, "further north."

The more northerly oriole thus was added to a list now totaling 737 species of North American birds that Savaloja has seen since he began birding as a teen-ager. Now 30, he is ranked 10th nationally by the American Birding Association, which has 6,000 members around the world.

There are more than 950 bird species in North America; Savaloja's goal is to see 800 before the end of the century. His Leitz binoculars are always in the car.

The country's top-ranked birder is Benton Basham, a Tennessee doctor who has 770 birds on his list. He's become something of a legend among birders for his chartering of airplanes at the ring of the phone. While it's not uncommon for some of the wealthier and less job-bound birders to literally chase a bird, Savaloja leads a more scheduled life. Each year, he leads a group to Attu, an island in the Aleutian chain, about 300 miles from Russia. It was on Attu in 1978 that he made the first green sandpiper sighting for North America. He spent three weeks in Japan last year, and is planning a trip to Venezuela or Mexico this winter.

"The only time I just leapt on a plane was to Texas in 1981 when a jabiru was sighted near Corpus Christi,' he says with a wistful grin.

The jabiru is a stork-like creature about 5 feet tall with a distinctive red throat. Savaloja arrived just after noon. At 2 o'clock, the jabiru took flight — and kept flying.

A group of birders arrived five minutes later. While there may have been some heartfelt commiseration, there no doubt was some quiet gloating, too.

Therein lies the difference between birding and bird-watching.

Bird-watching is a Sunday afternoon with a blanket near some backwater populated by mallards and shovelers with an occasional heron wafting in. It's a hike with timeouts for red-tailed hawks. It's calling the kids when the Canada geese honk over. It is casual, occasional.

"Birding, on the other hand, is an actual competitive sport," says Priscilla Tucker, executive editor of the association's magazine, Birding. "You can compete against yourself as well as against others. That's what makes it fun. And you've got to love it to keep doing it."

You have to love, for example, standing in a marsh at midnight, clicking together two quarters as you converge on a yellow rail. Clicking quarters is what humans do when they want to sound like a yellow rail.

The rail marked the beginning of Savaloja's national fame. It's an unusual bird to see anywhere in North America and he sighted it near Deerwood, in central Minnesota.

Avid birders traveled to Deerwood from across the country, asking Savaloja to lead them to this marsh. The reward was a bird so naturally fearless — or perhaps so amused — that birders could get close enough to pick it up.

Savaloja is a good person to lead such trips because he has a great deal of patience, says Ruth M. Carter, a fellow birder who recently moved from Minneapolis to Rochester. With 656 sightings to her credit, she is ranked 115th by the birding association. She's been on several trips with Savaloja "and he is so helpful. He tries to make sure every trip is worthwhile. He's really committed to birding, ever since he was a little boy."

Savaloja grew up in Deerwood. He began birding as a diversion while delivering papers for his father, a district circulation manager for the Minneapolis Star and Tribune. He even remembers his first bird, a pileated woodpecker. The diversion soon took on direction. He graduated from Crosby-Ironton High School and enrolled in the travel program at Brainerd Area Vocational Technical Institute with an eye toward combining his quest for birds with ready access to a mechanical means of migration. Now working at North Star Travel in Owatonna, he'd like to purvey his experience into his own international company for bird tours.

Forget the stereotypical safari shorts and scoutmaster's helmet, the image of Jane Hathaway stalking the wilds in search of a Beverly Hillbilly. Savaloja has the beefy build of a fullback and the grin of a successful hitchhiker. He is single, though he jokes about asking the women he dates if they'd like to stop and listen for whippoorwills.

The route to becoming a birder is as simple as looking up, he says. Up is where the birds are. No great revelation, which makes Savaloja wonder at times if people don't make birding harder than it really is. "A lot of people say, 'I've never seen an eagle in my life,' but this time of year, I see one or two a week," he says.

Yet even he wonders why he is so successful.

"I don't know. I ask myself sometimes, especially when I'm with some beginning birders who can't understand why they can't see this or that bird. They want to so badly. I guess it's just a skill I have."

Birding appeals to him because you can develop it into whatever you want it to be, he says, "And there's always someone I can call, no matter where I am, even if it's someone I've never met. You run into all these people who say, 'Well, if you're ever in California...'"

While the National Audubon Society, with a membership of more than 400,000 does more political lobbying of conservation issues than the American Birding Association, Savaloja says you hardly can be a birder without becoming aware of environmental issues.

"You begin to realize just how varied the habitats have to be for all these species," he says. "The destruction in Mexico and South America, the rain forests that are being destroyed — you just wonder what's going to happen."

UPDATE: Terry Savaloja has moved to Texas.

This looks like a job for — Fred the Fixer!

He's broken into more homes than any one man in Sioux Falls.

Thousands of locks have fallen prey to the painstaking probe of his pick, whether he works brazenly in broad daylight or under the cloak of darkness.

His best friends know him as Stanley Burkey—the guy who runs a quiet little shop on S. Grange Avenue. Others know him better as Fred the Fixer.

For more than 60 years, the little key shop has been the place to go—sheepishly—when you lock yourself in or out of home, car, bathroom or leg irons.

He's seen 'em all.

"Fred" was Burkey's father and started a repair shop back in 1918. Since there "weren't that many locks back then," most of the business was repair work and Fred soon gained a reputation for being able to fix anything, hence, Fred the Fixer.

Working up until the age of 84, Fred died in 1974, leaving the business to his son Stanley who, at 61, has 51 years of experience under his key chain.

The tales Burkey tells are a varied concoction of incidents born of a predicament that shows no favorites. Everyone is a potential victim.

"I suppose three or four times a week, I go out where there's a kid locked in the bathroom," he says. "But every once in a while there's a grown woman who does the same thing.

"Once a lady called up and asked if I would open up her mother's house because she hadn't heard from her in a few days. Found her dead in bed," he says, enjoying a listener's reaction.

"I've been called out on a few suicides, too, you know.

"Then there was the time I had to go to McKennan where they had a guy restrained in those leg iron things. They were too tight and his legs swelled up but the key wouldn't work so I had to cut 'em off with a drill, but it went pretty well.

"I did nick the flesh a little, though," he adds, his Ivy League cap lending a roguish humor to his words.

The stories roll out as he doodles on the brown wrapping paper taped to the desk top—a cheap, disposable message board for the addresses that are phoned in every day.

At night, things aren't that convenient. His biggest complaint is when people call him, then either pick the lock themselves or give up and leave without calling him back.

"When they wake me up at night, I'm doing good to get their address. I'm not that awake to get their names. So when I get there and they've left, all I can do is go back home to bed.

"Course, I swear a little on the way back."

With calls coming in from everyone and anyone, doesn't he wonder if maybe he's providing red carpet treatment for a crook?

"Oh, I wonder about that a lot; every time I go out," he says. "But there's really no way of telling. You don't carry around your car title, do you? And if you do, it's inside that locked up car."

When in doubt, Burkey has called on the police department for verification, especially if a call comes in after midnight. "Then I'm more skeptical." It has happened twice, though, that Burkey made keys for what turned out to be stolen cars, but that's not a bad record over 51 years.

"Didn't get paid for either one of them, either," he says, in a half-hearted effort to sound indignant.

While Burkey says he hasn't gotten rich locksmithing, he has earned a successful livelihood, with speed as the key ingredient.

"If you're not there in 10 or 15 minutes, forget it because they'll call someone else. You'd better be half-way there by the time you hang up the phone."

Such advice is being passed on to his 22-year-old daughter, Charlene, or Chick, who apparently will carry on the family tradition as Burkey and his wife, Athea, give some thought to slowing down.

He'll leave her plenty of business, though.

"You'd be surprised, in a town this size, how many houses aren't locked," he says, shaking his head.

UPDATE: Stanley Burkey is now retired, but Fred the Fixer still goes on managed by the original Fred's granddaughter and her husband.

"What..."

Canning meat to feed the world

FREEMAN, S.D.—Orville Langerock drops his shoulder for leverage, digging into the huge vat of steaming meat with what looks like a boat paddle. Around him, other men are slicing great chunks of beef into steak-size pieces that are, in turn, ground into one-inch morsels that are, in turn, dumped into the stewing vat.

The dank smell of moist, raw meat fills the air of Weins' Auto Mart converted for a few days into a canning factory.

"Aren't you glad you live in America?" Langerock asks, biceps straining as he stirs a coffee can's worth of salt into the beef.

It is not a satirical crack poking fun at their makeshift assembly line, but a heartfelt belief confirmed by the thought, word and deed of everyone else in the room.

These people, representing 22 area churches, are glad they're living in America and aim to share their good fortune with the world's starving millions who have never seen a pound of meat, much less the almost 28,000 pounds that were canned this week in Freeman.

"We all believe in the Scripture that says, 'Give and it shall be given unto you,'" Henry Zanter says, taking a break from slicing beef.

All the beef canned Monday and the pork canned Tuesday was bought with community donations "of more than $40,000, cash money," Horb Schmidt says. "And the checks are still coming in."

The meat canning project began in 1975 when about 15,000 pounds of meat were canned. This year, chairman Jerry Graber expects to can 26,000 pounds.

Last year, meat made available by the Mennonite Central Committee for world export totaled 415,846 pounds from all the canning projects.

The project is made possible by a tractor-trailer that travels across the United States with canning equipment to be used by communities preparing food for world relief.

The outfit is owned by the central committee of the Mennonite Church, but the project in Freeman attracts everyone—Baptists, Presbyterians, Lutherans as well as Mennonites.

The only thing the 25 communities served by the trailer need to provide is the meat and the labor.

Both were in good supply this week.

If there is a masculine counterpart to the quilting bee, it must be a line of men who fill the cans with meat after its turn in the stewing vat.

Gossip is exchanged and world problems are solved as the tin cans travel from the hands of the filler to the packer to the sealer to the catcher to the stacker.

Iran is the word on most lips as they wonder whether a military act is the solution or what Billy Carter has to say about it.

And there's always the kidding.

"Come on, can man," they tease the guy who falls a bit behind lining up the empty cans. "Hey, don't breathe too much of this air because it's sterile," another says, drawing laughter from the men working in the trailer open to the chilly air outdoors.

Actually, they add, all the meat is government-approved and a meat inspector is on hand to ensure the freshness and quality of the product.

Harold Schreiner, meat inspector at John Morrell & Co., drew this year's duty that consists mostly of trying to act busy while monitoring a group of people who probably keep the space under their sinks cleaner than most of us keep our living rooms.

"It's going to be a long day," Schreiner says, smiling, "but it's a fantastic project. It's really hard to imagine the type of thing that's going on over in Iran, and then see a project like this."

Indeed, an ordinary, slightly messy project like canning meat is not often thought of as a religious experience, but there is a sense of that special brotherhood in Freeman when this time of year rolls around.

Women roll up their shirtsleeves and wrap their hair in kerchiefs for a marathon session in tubs of dishwater, cleaning the steamed cans so the label can be pasted on.

In the corner, homemade salami sandwiches and brownies are piled high for the lunchbreak. It's a contrast of plenty that doesn't go unnoticed.

"All of this," Adena Pullman said, reaching toward the small aluminum mountain for another can to wash, "and it's still not enough to go around."

Originally published 12-7-79 as "Many hands make light work of canned meat."

UPDATE: The canned meat project goes on, but the location has moved to Marion, S.D., a few miles from Freeman.

When you want cod in the worst way

BERESFORD, S.D. — When Harold Tollefson died earlier this year, his heart no doubt was slightly bruised from watching what had become of his baby.

Ah, if he could see her now, he'd probably order second helpings.

(Yah shoore, you betcha.)

Tollefson was a man who knew his community and knew its appetite. When he shrewdly founded Tolly's Cafe just as the interstate highway was being slapped down west of town, he created an institution.

The business, unfortunately, went the way of his retirement. In fact, before Mark Nielsen returned in January to his hometown, the place had been boarded up.

Nielsen may never be another Tolly, but he knows his community and knows its appetite. He knows what a slab of smelly codfish waved under the nose of any self-respecting Scandinavian will do for business.

Perhaps self-respecting is the wrong term to use when speaking of ingesting this particular item. In this city about 40 miles south of Sioux Falls, however, self-respect takes a back seat to tradition on Monday nights because Monday nights mean ludefisk.

A digression to explain the nature of this Scandinavian delicacy: There are many stories regarding the origin of this dish, most of them having to do with wooden barrels, back porches and errant dogs.

Actually, ludefisk is cod that has been dried, then reconstituted by soaking it in a lye solution. It then is rinsed in water for several days and scrubbed until it gets the slightly rubbery consistency that characterizes the white, almost translucent fish.

Cooking it is a simple matter: Boil in salted water, being careful not to overcook it to mush nor undercook it to slime.

Serving ludefisk, however, can inspire as much controversy as the fish itself. Some prefer it with butter, some with white sauce, some with allspice in their white sauce, some without, some with a mustard sauce, some with it wrapped in their lefse and held together with some mashed potatoes.

Tolly's tries to please almost everyone, although you have to bring your own allspice.

Otherwise, the Monday meal carries all the marks of becoming a tradition: a choice of three salads. mashed potatoes, a vegetable ("preferably something colorful"), lefse, flatbread and baked Swedish rice pudding laced with raisins.

Surprisingly, the tradition is being established by a man who just turned 26 and who admittedly is a bit ignorant of the fish.

Unpacking a 50-pound box of Viking Genuine Norwegian Ludefisk, Nielsen says he's never looked at enough of the stuff to know whether it's good or not, "but Melvie says it's excellent."

Melvie Olsen is the key to the banquet's success, a ringer brought in from neighboring Centerville. She's been cooking ludefisk since she was 15 years old and, although she doesn't want her age in the paper, suffice it to say she has about 55 years of experience.

"It was always my job to cook it for all the relatives," she says in a slight Swedish accent that she thinks she doesn't have. "I enjoy doing it, I really do, but you have to watch it very carefully."

Gingerly, she pokes the five or six chunks of fish snagged in a cheesecloth bag. Although she admits that ludefisk is an acquired taste, she is a traditionalist at heart. When a visitor tells her that she eats some fish every Christmas to make her grandma happy, Mrs. Olsen shakes her fork and deems that very good.

They could probably use such a pep talk at the cafe's front door, for it is there that the ludefisk debates are waged between the eaters, who are shuffled into the dining room on the right, and the non-eaters, who are seated in the booths to the left.

"Oh, I can eat it if I have to," a left-sider says. "Like if I haven't had lunch for three days."

Right-siders, in the meantime, are forming a waiting line.

"There's a little more of a party atmosphere on these nights," Nielsen says, "Everyone — the people, my crew — everyone seems to have more fun."

Indeed, Nielsen first planned to offer the feed through December, but now intends to keep it up through January and February, "because some people have suggested very nicely that they'll break my neck if I don't."

"It's something that's fading as the generations go by. It's easier for an older couple to come here than doing all the rigamarole because there is a lot of rigamarole involved.

"I think it probably reminds them of home."

Originally published 12-21-80 as "Ludefisk in Beresford brings diners, debaters."

UPDATE: The new owner of Tolly's Cafe, Howie Pedersen, says he will continue the tradition of ludefisk dinner on Saturday nights from November through January.

Bringing in the ice. For many it was the first time; for most it was the last time. (ARGUS LEADER photo by Frank Klock. Reprinted by permission.)

The ice-harvest revival

SPIRIT LAKE, Iowa—There was an ominous snap, then the ice abruptly gave way, slipping Keith Frost knee-deep into the frigid green waters.

"Well, now it's official," one bystander shouted over the laughter as Frost clambered up onto the ledge of ice again.

The ice harvest had begun.

More than 200 people, waddling around in snowmobile suits or slipsliding across the icy expanse of Big Spirit Lake, gathered Sunday to watch an art lost to time, progress and Frigidaire.

For many, it was the first time they'd seen an ice harvest. For all, it probably will be the last.

Ice harvesting, or "making ice" as the old-timers say, was a major industry here back at the turn of the century up until the 1950s, with Spirit Lake ice sent to New York or Chicago or St. Louis. Or to the Johnson family's icebox around the corner.

Sunday, that industry was revived as men took up the same ragged-tooth saws and pronged sticks that were used nearly a half century ago.

Bill Eich manned one saw for the first time in his life, quickly shedding his parka from the exertion of cutting through 2 1/2 feet of ice.

"Sure makes you appreciate your automatic ice maker at home," he said, his beard dewy with sweat.

It's hard work.

It starts early in the winter as crews keep the ice swept clear of insulating snow so the surface freezes thick. Then 40 squares are marked out and a channel dug linking the ice field to the shore.

The two-foot-square chunks are sawed apart on two sides, then chiseled free to bob in the water as pronged sticks guide them toward the channel. There, an ice tong attached to a rope locks around the block and a draft horse pulls the 500-pound chunks up a ramp and onto a wagon.

The ice is trucked to a shed where it's packed in sawdust to await use. In Spirit Lake's case, the ice will be unearthed June 23, when the town celebrates its centennial.

Ed Hummel, one of the dozen veteran ice harvesters there, remembered the days back in 1913 when they'd get 25 cents for a wagonload of ice.

"We could make $5 a day on good days," he said. "It was good work during the winter when we didn't have much to do on the farm.

"Course, back then we didn't have programs to pay us for doing nothing, either," he said, cocking one eyebrow.

Despite the saws and picks and tons of ice being jockeyed through the frigid depths, Hummel said ice harvesting isn't so dangerous, although he remembers getting his toes smashed one time when an ice chunk slipped.

"I never seen anything very fatal, though," he said.

Another veteran, Jim Bonsall, came up just then and the two compared notes on the performance of the rookies and haggled about how thick ice should be before it's cut.

"This is the thickest I've ever seen the ice here," Hummel said, "but they're cutting the blocks way too big."

Bonsall, however, thought they were doing OK "considering what they have to work with," and recalled the days back in the 1930's when he'd take two or three weeks off from school to make ice.

"Ice cost about a cent a pound back in those days," he said. But it could be quite a process to deliver.

Bonsall said the ice wagon would come and pull up to the chute on the side of each house. There, a rope would be tied to the ice blocks and run over a pulley and through the house to a team of horses waiting on the other side. At the sound of a whistle, the horses would pull the ice up the chute and into the house.

Ice was harvested on Big Spirit Lake until 1951 when electricity finally took over for good.

Jerry Stukey, of the SnoRiders snowmobile club who sponsored the event, said the only training Sunday's ice men got was a 1937 film that a local man had made.

"And I was surprised at the number of people who'd stop in and volunteer information about how to do it," he said, gulping down a cup of coffee.

"These guys who worked the early harvests are really getting a buzz out of scrutinizing this today," he said. "This is really for them."

Just then, Frost came up and tapped him on the shoulder. "I'm going home to change," said the unlucky harvester shaking the water from boots. "Be back in a bit."

Doing the hogs

LESTER, Iowa — The thick planks, pale blood-pink deep within the grain, shudder as the side of pork slides off a man's shoulders and lands hard, jarring them from the barrels supporting the ends.

Talk of stopping for coffee floats through air made clammy as warm-animal flesh mingles steamily with a February snowstorm.

Toward the rear of the cement block building on Jacob Wulf's farm hang 17 hog carcasses, their hind leg tendons strung through meat hooks. A rosy ham can be glimpsed beneath a layer of fat yet to be trimmed away.

The 18th carcass is on the makeshift table, grasped by thick farmers' hands that slice muscle from bone as deftly as if they were sitting at the supper table:

They've done it for as long as many can remember, do it because their parents and grandparents did.

Seven families from the Lester area, in extreme northwestern Iowa, set aside three days last week to "do the hogs."

It's a tradition that goes beyond any sentimental memories that "this is the way grandpa used to do it." Instead, it is more firmly based in the practical concern that meat locker costs, along with everything else, are rising and they can do just as good'a job themselves.

"The way things are going, we might start doing our beef, too," Wulf says, barely smiling.

Besides, they finally relent, it's fun when the families of Verlyn Kellenberger, Art Knobloch, Raymond Luthi, Bob Matzen, George Meyer, Raymond Meyer and Jacob Wulf get together and visit, helped out by neighbors that just seem to happen by.

And you've never tasted such sausage or chewed such bacon as comes out of those hours sandwiched in between chores.

Nor have you heard such jokes.

Roy Metzger, spying a newcomer, brings a bucket full of what looks like — oh, it is — pigs' eyes.

"Our wives put one of those in our pockets so when we go to town, they say they've got an eye on us."

As one wag said, you only believe 10 percent of what you hear when these folks get together.

The day begins about 8 a.m. when the pigs are shot and bled, then scalded to remove the hair. They then are carefully gutted — the small intestines, livers, hearts and other organs saved to make liver sausage.

The hogs' heads are the first order of business as whiskers are scraped off, ears removed (they go into the sausage, too) and meat cut away from the jawbone.

The eyes, at a schoolteacher's request, go into a bucket for a science project.

Over the bloodied table flies talk of farm policies and market prices, newspaper delivery and basketball games.

The rasp of knives against files carries above the conversation.

The women busy themselves back in the corner, scraping clean the small intestines with action that seems too vigorous for what looks like gossamer-thin tissue. "They're tougher than you think," Lauretta Knobloch says, hair swept out of her face by a kerchief. Indeed, the hollow tube is surprisingly elastic and hard to puncture.

"It's getting so expensive to go to a locker anymore," she says of the community effort.

But how do they keep the meat from 18 hogs — indistinguishable in their butchered state — from going to the wrong person?

"Oh, we let the men take care of that," one woman says, smiling.

The same question posed to the men draws similar smiles before any answer comes.

"We try to keep them batched in tubs," one says, but you get the impression it's not a serious offense if a ham gets switched.

After all, they know they're all good farmers feeding their hogs better corn raised in even finer Iowa fields. They trust each other, or they wouldn't be working together like this every year.

It's a cooperative effort, Wulf says.

"Ray Metzger and I have the meat grinder, the Meyer brothers have the saw," he says, looking down the table lined with overalled bodies. "They've done it as long as they've farmed."

Later, Wulf wields the knife when the time comes to cut the ham from the half-carcass. Purposefully, he guides the blade around the hindquarter, heaving over the ham so another can cut off the fat and sending the bony length on to the big white DoAll saw to be cut into roasts and spareribs.

The fat will be rendered the next day, heated until it melts down, then strained into jars. There's nothing like a piecrust made with good lard. Absolutely nothing.

Sausage-making will occupy most of the following day as the scraps and innards are cooked up and ground, spiced and forced into the small intestines.

The hams will be smoked at the locker, as will the bacon. Modern technology comes in handy, sometimes.

But chances are good it won't encroach much further into the lives of these people when it comes to putting up meat. Looking around at the skill displayed, the easy way they work together, there's no reason why it should.

"You know, this is no lie, John Morrell has tried to get this gang to come and work for years," Roy Metzger says, then clears his throat to leave no doubt there's not only a frog down there, but a lot of bull besides.

Just some of that 90 percent you're not supposed to believe.

UPDATE: They're still doing the hogs at Lester as they have for years, with most of the same families participating.

Irene Colling and her art. "A straight line isn't a straight line." (ARGUS LEADER photo by John Danicic Jr., reprinted by permission.)

Art among the haystacks

HOWARD, S.D. — Art, like love, is where you find it — even if it's in the middle of a section of Lake County farmland.

Peeking between haystacks and fenceposts is an airy art gallery frequented most often by pigeons and cattle, but open to anyone driving down the gravel road narrowed by a recent snowstorm.

The walls of the gallery are barbed wire fences, the paint ings done on huge sheets of corrugated steel. Irene Colling is the artist-in-residence and the curator is a rancher with a vision as big as the South Dakota sky above.

Ernest W. Shove commissioned the murals on four of his ranch buildings northwest of Howard, their colors a vibrant splash against the bleached white of ankle-deep snow.

There's a pheasant swooping around the curve of a corncrib, a rainbow tracing the arched roofline of a Quonset hut. A pioneer steers his plow across the wall of one shed, while a homesteader makes his way across the prairie on another.

The murals are Shove's way of paying homage to the existence he's found here in South Dakota.

"This quality of life we have here, it's important it be preserved," he says in measured phrases. "You have beautiful pictures in your home that just a few people see, so why not have them outside where everybody can see them?"

With that thought in mind, he called on Mrs. Colling.

"He knew I had been selling paintings around here so he asked if I would paint a picture on the side of one of his buildings—just a little picture, I thought," she says, smiling at the memory. "I didn't know he meant the whole building."

Shove, a rancher since he retired in 1955 from a job as rural mail carrier, wants the murals to commemorate the pioneer, so the first project was a man breaking the prairie while a flock of geese fly overhead.

"My father homesteaded here, about a mile north of Howard," the stocky Shove says. "I feel that these should be a tribute."

Mrs. Colling started with a freehand drawing on the side of the shed, and slowly began to realize what she'd taken on.

"The hardest thing to do is get the basic sketch on," she says of the immense panoramas. "You're working up close and can't tell what it looks like so you have to stop and run 20 feet back to look all the time."

Further complicating matters is the corrugated surface of the sheet metal, "because a straight line isn't a straight line. It's in and out, in and out."

Each mural—she's done one a year for four years—takes about two weeks to complete and uses about six gallons of latex paint. Friends help paint in the basic sky and ground colors, leaving her to work out the details.

She paints from perches high in the bucket of a front-end loader, straddles ladders propped against the building and climbs precarious towers built from planks and sawhorses.

Petite, bespectacled, with short brown hair, the conservative Mrs. Colling doesn't look like the avant-garde artist one expects to find in a studio where the only background music is the moo of cows.

Her fee ranges from $200-250, but that depends on the subject and her children.

"To a degree, I work by the hour, but I take the kids along and I'm always stopping and starting, depending on what they need. And I'm getting much faster, too."

That's a good thing, since the neighbors have begun asking if she'd turn their farmyards into open-air art exhibits.

Next year's project is a bucking horse on the side of a corn crib, but Shove is thinking even further ahead. The only trouble is that he's running out of canvas, er, buildings.

What I'd like to do is have a whole pioneer threshing bee with all the wagons and horses, but I don't have a building big enough," he says, then grins, "I'll have to put one up special."

Originally published 12-3-79 as "Art among the haystacks."

UPDATE: Irene Collings continues to paint murals in the area. Ernest Shove died in the early 1980s.

Wooden horses — coming 'round again

HOPKINS, Minn. — On those unbearably literal days when fantasy seems in short supply, think of Ray Bahmer and take heart.

His task is preserving the fantasy of the carrousel, that ancient diversion of wooden horses galloping to uncharted

Kenny Bahmer, on the left, and his brother Ray put the finishing touches on a carved steed. Watch for the pink eyelashes. (STAR TRIBUNE photo by Darlene Pfister. Reprinted by permission.)

lands, yet pausing for your dismount just where you began. Among the careening coasters and churning octopi, a carnival's carrousel is not so much an anachronism as a reprieve for mind as well as body.

The carrousel in question is the one at Valleyfair Family Amusement Park in Shakopee, the one that since 1926 spun at the Excelsior Amusement Park until it closed in 1973. Now, 60 years old, it needed some deep healing. Bahmer won the bidding.

To most people, he's Ray, the guy who owns The Furniture Gallery in Hopkins, finishing chairs in need of fresh cane and buffets in need of new varnish. It's a skill he regards as art, exposing a wood grain left for lost or weaving rushes to suit a seat.

Now, with a grin, he calls himself Dr. Ray. With his glue, a rickety horse is reborn. Under his chisel, a mane re-emerges. Each horse, of malleable aspen, commands at least 20 hours of labor, what with stripping varnish, strengthening legs, gluing tails, applying and sanding seven or eight coats of primer, then painting by spray gun and hand — three coats — before sealing with clear enamel.

Little wonder it's difficult to keep his mind on fantasy.

"This is the most scientific thing I've done," Bahmer says, sounding slightly exasperated. "For instance, the glue has to dry 48 hours at just the right temperature and if you don't give it 48 hours, the molecular bond isn't made and you have to resort to mechanical bonds. But if it was all fun, they wouldn't call it work."

If he forgets about fantasy, "the people at Valleyfair remind me," he says, laughing. "My problem is that they're not real horses, but as an artist, I want them to look like real horses. I want to brush in muscles and stipple the saddles. But I can't do that. I can't make them too real. They're supposed to be fantasy."

This battle against reality no doubt has contributed to the lunacy that prevails at times in the old clapboard building. The horse with the broken leg has been christened Skippy. "We built little corrals for them, too," says Bahmer's brother, Kenny. "You have to do something to stay sane."

Sentiment creeps in. This was the merry-go-round Bahmer rode as a kid. He may have outgrown it for a time when the dance pavilion beckoned across the way, but he's at an age —

35 — when the past is distant enough to be relived. There are further motivations: The furniture he finishes, the '68 Firebird convertible he restored all speak to one belief: "I just hate seeing old things go to waste."

Such reverence is all too rare, says Frederick Fried, a folk art historian in New York City and expert on carrousels who co-founded the National Carrousel Association.

"How do carrousels stand today? Very perilously. Combines of collectors are forming, offering huge prices to carrousel owners, then breaking them up to sell as art objects," Fried says. In the past year alone, 38 carrousels have been dismantled, he says, one with four rows of horses recently selling piece by piece for $480,000.

In response, the association takes its case to children and parents — and to cities that have sold their carrousels and now have residents clamoring for another. "We tell them you can't go out and get it again and not pay four to five times what you sold it for."

Fried sees a renaissance in carrousels.

"People are getting very excited," he says. "Think of it! A carrousel has painting, sculpture, movement and music — all the arts in one. In 12 years, our organization has grown to 1,000 members. We've made the public realize a great work of art." Unfortunately, he adds, publicity that carrousels are being dismantled also makes the public aware that such memorabilia is available: "I hope we haven't created our own death knell."

The carrousel's origins are unknown, although a similar device is part of an early Byzantine bas-relief. The word "carrousel" came into use from the ancient Italian word *garosello*, meaning "little war," and describes a serious game played by Turkish horsemen in the 12th century. The French, ever sensuous, turned it into a lavish event in which clay balls filled with scented water were thrown between horsemen, perfuming the "enemy."

"The wind would waft the scent to the sidelines filled with spectators and everyone would sniff approvingly, identifying their side by the fragrance," Fried writes in his book, *A Pictorial History of the Carrousel.*

One event was tilting at the *quintain*, or catching a brass ring on a lance. The carrousel began to take on the form we know today when someone thought of suspending wooden horses from arms radiating from a center pole on which knights could practice their spearing.

Men and mules got a break from providing the motive power in 1832 when a geared cranking device was developed. In 1865, steam power was harnessed, a concept that was improved upon by the center truck, a rotating frame that could support great weight.

This opened the door to elaborate carving — a style some have called Fairground Rococo — and by 1890, carving carrousel horses was a highly skilled business providing fulltime employment. The popularity of amusement parks led such people as Henry B. Auchy to found in 1903 the Philadelphia Toboggan Co., makers of the Valleyfair carrousel. (Toboggans, by the way, were what roller coasters were called: they formed the bulk of the company's business.)

Bahmer is in awe of that era: "I just can't fathom how the guy started the company, how he found so many talented people. I mean, they were all experts who did this. The guy who picked out the wood in the forest said, 'I want this tree and that tree and that tree.' And the quality of carving is unbelievable. You can see the veins in their faces. And the wild-eyed look in some of them!" Credit Frank Carretta, a carver whose work came to personify the Philadelphia Toboggan Co. An Italian immigrant, he joined the company in 1924 and within 12 months, became a master carver, entering the domain of creating heads and tails. Bodies were left to apprentices. His flamboyant designs earned him a place in the carrousel-carvers Hall of Fame in Sarasota, Fla.

Today, the Philadelphia Toboggan Co. still makes roller coasters, but built its 94th and last carrousel in 1934.

"Now we make parts for them" said company president Sam High. He tries to keep track of how many of their carrousels still run, "but it's hard since they're getting broken up so quickly. Some guy thinks he'd like a carrousel horse in his office or a business wants one in their lobby and there they go."

It's a turnaround from the 1950s, when High joined the company. "They were junking carrousels then. We had an attic full of old horses that someone took off our hands for $200 — and we were glad to get the $200." A revival began in 1955 with the construction of Disneyland, followed by Six Flags Over Texas in the 1960s. "Next thing you know, theme parks are getting built all over and they all wanted a carrousel and the price started to go."

Today, old carrousel horses bring up to $35,000, according to High, who adds the Valleyfair 48-horse carrousel likely cost between $17,000 and $18,000 in 1926. Some parks with old carrousels, knowing their value, have sold the original horses and replaced them with the new fiberglass or aluminum models, High says, but at their own peril: "A small park just outside of Philadelphia did that not too long ago and public opinion just turned against them. There may have been some other reasons, but they ended up closing down."

Valleyfair keeps the horses in annual cosmetic order, such as painting where the stirrups rub, says mechanical supervisor Jim Avis, but loosening joints prompted this more ambitious restoration project. Bahmer has finished eight horses; more may be completed as funding permits.

When the park opens May 10, though, you'll be able to tell which of the horses have felt Bahmer's touch. Artist that he is, he couldn't resist leaving his mark, paying his tribute to fantasy: His are the ones with pink eyelashes.

UPDATE: Ray Bahmer has moved to Chicago, Ill.

"Where..."

Of flesh and stone

TYLER, Minn.— Centuries ago, the hollow clunk of rock striking rock echoed across the treeless plains surrounding a gully streaked with pinkish stone.

Today, the echo has a metallic ring that rebounds off the willows growing here near what now is the city of Pipestone.

For instead of the sharp stone of his ancestors, Dick Bryan clutches a sledgehammer to quarry chunks of the dusky rose stone from its quartzite bed.

It's a craft Bryan has learned from his father, who learned it from his, and so on perhaps as far back as 1200 A.D. Now Bryan is teaching his teen-age son and daughter the tradition of carving the sacred rock called pipestone.

The Bryan clan of Tyler is one of only 50 American Indian families in the United States which has a permit to quarry the stone at the Pipestone National Monument.

"I think it's coming back now," Bryan, a registered Sisseton Sioux, says of the carving. "It was almost gone back in the '40s. I think there were only about three who quarried.

"Now, there's 50."

The permits are available to those who are at least one-quarter registered Indian and prohibit the use of any modern tools to quarry the stone.

So each fall, the family shoulders picks, shovels, brooms and hammers and travels the 20 miles south to the monument, where Bryan is maintenance man, to begin the back-breaking task of unearthing the pipestone.

According to legend, pipestone was formed when a great flood threatened to destroy the earth. To escape, the tribes assembled on the Coteau des Prairies, a striking geographical feature of highlands dividing the watersheds of the Mississippi and Missouri rivers.

But the water continued to rise and covered the tribes, converting their flesh to red stone.

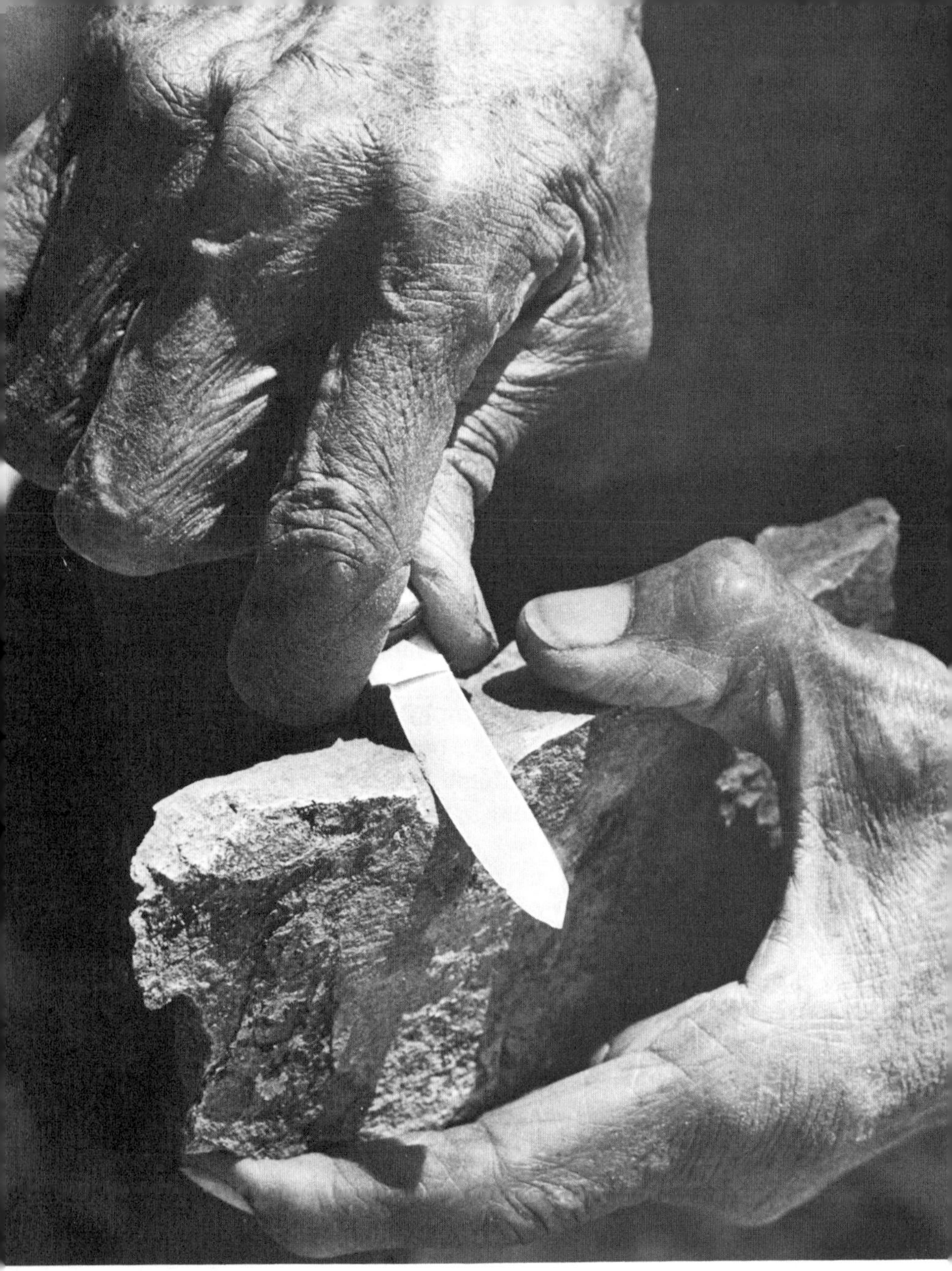

Form out of chaos. Standing Eagle shapes a slab of pipestone with a pocket knife. "I thought there was something more in that stone, something I could get out." (ARGUS LEADER photo by John Danicic Jr., reprinted by permission.)

To scientists, the formation is a compressed metamorphic clay called catlinite. To Indians, however, the rock symbolizes the souls of their forefathers.

But imbedded under 14 feet of solid Sioux quartzite, it takes a lot of soul-searching to get down to the 1- to 2-foot vein of softer pipestone.

"It's kinda nice down there in the fall, y'know. No bugs, kinda cool," Bryan says, crossing his arms across a chest broadened by hours of swinging a sledgehammer.

Bryan says he is able to remove only about two feet each year of the yard-wide slab of pipestone that runs through his 50-foot dig. His area is called The Spotted Quarry, so named for the distinctive pink mottling through the deeper rose of the stone there.

But that's enough rock to keep him busy through the winter months since he's switched his emphasis from the traditional pipe-making to more innovative sculpture-carving.

"I don't know. I guess I felt like I wasn't doing enough with just the pipes," he says, although he estimates carving about 3,000 of them in his 25 years at the craft.

"I thought there was something more in that stone, something I could get out.

"Now, I think I'm satisfied."

But that satisfaction is a hard-won prize due to the painstaking nature of carving the stone.

"You see, pipestone is only about as hard as a fingernail," Bryan says, demonstrating the tedious scraping he does to transform the raw chunks into the stylized sculptures that fill his home studio.

"I've carved horses that have taken two or three months only to have the ear break off with the final few scrapes," he says with a lame smile. "If you don't think that's heartbreaking..."

His first sculpture, and the one "I'll always be the most excited about," is a replica of the famous painting, "The End of the Trail," depicting an Indian warrior bent wearily in his saddle.

The deep maroon glow reflected in the muscled shoulder seems to soften the stone and disguises its 17-pound heft.

Bryan achieves the distinctive burnish by dipping the statue in melted beeswax, then plunging it into cold water to set the glaze.

The project took four months of Bryan's off-hours, not counting the time it took to quarry the stone. For that, the foot-high statue carries a $2,400 price tag.

"No, I'm not getting many buyers," he says in reaction to an observer's raised eyebrows. "But I don't know if I'm all that anxious to give some of this up, either."

Most of what Bryan makes, he trades for anything from ancient Indian relics to hay for his horses. His work is displayed in Sioux Falls at Jim Savage's Western Art Gallery and in Brookings at the Good Earth Craft Shop.

Bryan operates under the name Whirl Wind, which his grandfather gave to him in the Indian tradition.

But the story behind it is hardly the romantic folklore one would expect of his grandfather seeing a great funnel of wind churn across the prairie at the moment of his grandson's birth.

"No, I guess I was always running around never stopping, getting into everything," Bryan says somewhat sheepishly. "Sort of drove'em crazy, I guess."

Although he's got enough work to keep him busy through the winter, Bryan probably will make one more trip down to the quarry, largely under the urgings of his 70-year-old father who, according to Bryan, still swings a mighty hammer.

The question arises, however, that with 50 families all chipping away at the fixed amount of pipestone—a vein that has given way to the chiselings of centuries—how long will the supply of sacred stone last?

"There's a saying about that," Bryan says, thoughtfully scratching his head. "If 1 million Indians gathered and worked every day for 1,000 years, they still wouldn't get all of it."

Originally published 12-11-78 as "Centuries-old tradition continues at Pipestone."

How 2,000-year-old cheese came to a Minnesota cave

FARIBAULT, Minn. — Felix M. Frederiksen's wife, Dorothy, was a fan of Robert Louis Stevenson, especially the pirate tales he spun in *Treasure Island.* And that is how Treasure Cave Blue Cheese got its name.

No marketing studies, no consumer psychographics. That's how business was done half a century ago in Faribault when Frederiksen founded Treasure Cave, the oldest producer of blue cheese in this country.

The name fits. Within the sandstone caves dug into the Straight River bluffs is a treasure of sorts. Fat wheels of blue cheese, piquant and slate-veined, lie in the cool gloom, ripening in a manner that can be duplicated above ground but with less efficiency and, face it, less romance.

Treasure Cave's product is "outstanding," according to an article about blue cheese in the December issue of Bon Appetit. Faribault's caves, it said, were given new life when "an enterprising cheesemaker saw a potential American equivalent to Roquefort's underground chambers."

Cave-aged French Roquefort probably is the most famous of blue cheeses, followed by English Stilton and Italian Gorgonzota. American blues are less known but gaining in popularity, partly because of aggressive marketing by Treasure Cave and other producers.

Aggressiveness is not the word that comes to mind as you pull up to what appears a modest country creamery. Most of the first-place ribbons displayed in the small retail area are from the Minnesota State Fair and they've lapsed in posting their latest wins for four or five years now. Nor have they gotten around to putting the sign back on the roof after some remodeling work a few years ago — which may be just as well because they don't give tours anymore for reasons of sanitation, safety and security.

And, despite the cold sheen of stainless steel and the antiseptic white coats worn by the plant's 57 employees, there is an easy familiarity with the product and the premises. Human hands still rub each wheel with salt or package it in shiny foil.

When the cave walls need more whitewash, it's done with a bucket and paintbrush.

Each year, these caves play womb to millions of pounds of cheese. Plant manager Ralph Stuart declined to be more specific on volume, explaining that cheesemaking is a competitive business. One reason is that people are eating more cheese. Per capita consumption of what the U.S. Department of Agriculture calls American cheeses — such as Cheddar, Colby and Monterrey Jack — increased from 7.8 pounds in 1972 to 12.2 pounds in 1985.

The grocery store's cheese sections also have grown from being full of long yellow bricks to offering slabs of creamy Brie and herbed Camembert. "As American consumers' tastes become more diversified, the consumption of specialty cheese no longer is associated with a particular socioeconomic strata," said Stuart, an affable man whose sturdy frame betrays the taste-testing aspects of his job.

The biting flavor and moldy appearance of blue cheese may place it in the category of an acquired taste. According to the USDA, consumption of blue cheese in 1985 was .16 pounds per capita — unchanged from 1972, although there are, of course, more capitas out there today.

The history of blue cheese extends to the first century. Legend has it that a shepherd forgot his lunch in one of the caves in the Rouergue region of southern France. A month later, he found the cheese had molded — or ripened, depending on your point of view. He tasted it, liked it and mistake became marvel.

These were not just any caves, mind you — lunch forgotten in other caves simply dried out. These formed when the 3,000-foot Mount Cambalou collapsed upon itself, producing an environment of 45 degrees and 95 percent humidity that was conducive to the growth of the mold *penicillium roqueforti*. Today, only those cheeses ripened in the Mount Cambalou caves may legally carry the name Roquefort. They are further distinguished by being made only from the milk of sheep.

Cows, mostly Holsteins, give the milk that becomes the blue cheese of Faribault's caves. Once heated, it's poured into 15,000-pound-capacity vats into which the mold spores and something called enzyme coagulant is added. (By the way, Stuart said people allergic to penicillin are not allergic to blue cheese because *penicillium roqueforti* is a different spore.)

It then thickens into what resembles a huge dish of custard. This curd gets sliced into tiny cubes with tools called wire harps — fine wires strung between stainless steel tines that a worker pulls through the curd. It ends up looking like a tub of unmarked dice.

When this is stirred, though, a pool of yellowish liquid comes to the top as the curds sink to the bottom. This whey is drained off (it's dried and sold as by-product for food ingredients) and the curd is sent up a conveyor belt and into 8-inch-round forms. The curds settle overnight to form firm wheels of cheese which then are rubbed with salt to extract even more moisture. Each wheel then is sent through a machine that stabs it three times to provide tiny air spaces in which the mold can grow.

That's really all there is to it.

Or all that man can do. The rest is up to nature. Specifically, the caves.

It was a special sort of cave that Felix Frederiksen, he of the wife who liked swashbucklers, was looking for when he came to Minnesota with the dream of making blue cheese.

"Frederiksen served in France during World War I and became enamored of Roquefort cheese," Stuart said. The Wisconsin native was on his way to check out some caves in St. Peter when he saw a burned-out building and a cave entrance next to the river bluffs in Faribault. It was the old Godfrey Fleckenstein Brewery, founded in 1854. After it went out of business, the building was used for manufacturing lamps and furniture until it was gutted by fire.

The caves met Frederiksen's specifications: a steady temperature below 55 degrees and 90 percent humidity. Some artificial refrigeration is needed to maintain the curing and aging caves at optimum temperatures, but adjusting for a dozen degrees is more economic than regulating above-ground temperatures, and the proper humidity is free. He bought the property in 1935, renovated it and in 1936 the first blue cheese entered the caves.

These are not craggy bat-filled caves of Tom Sawyer's adventures, but whitewashed arched halls about 14 feet wide and 18 feet high. The Gothic arch shape of the ceilings better distributes the overburden — the stuff that could collapse — and thus far has been successful in that task.

The architecture of the caves has an added benefit of sorts, Stuart said. Once stocked with cheese, the corridors are too narrow to allow forklifts, so there are no whines and beeps disturbing the sepulchral silence.

The flip side is that all the stacking and unstacking is done by hand, but that too is a kind of tradition. While the original cave was natural, the rest have been dug by hand. "I understand that back in Frederiksen's day, when sales were down or it was a slow time, the employees would dig new caves with picks and shovels," Stuart said. "The new caves we've dug with jackhammers, but it's still strenuous work."

Over the years, Frederiksen's biggest clients were meatpacking companies such as George Hormel & Co., and Swift & Co., which distributed the cheese with their other products. When Frederiksen retired in 1966, Swift bought the company. In 1984, Beatrice Foods acquired Swift.

Today, the cheese leaves the plant as wheels, cubes and crumbles after having been aged about 100 days. Federal standards require that blue cheese be aged 60 days. The longer the aging, the more flavorful the cheese. So far, it all remains in the United States, although Stuart said he has received an inquiry from somewhere in Cancun asking about distribution.

In the retail sales area, Stuart broke open a box of crackers and lifted the lid protecting a chunk of cheese. "This one isn't quite as blue as we'd like them to be," he said, munching critically. Why? It's difficult to say.

"We tend to put everything into scientific perspectives and measurable quantities," he explained, topping one more cracker. "But there still is an art to making cheese. It's still an art."

A long way from anywhere

PIERRE, S.D. — As a friend said as we crossed this city's limits, Pierre is a lot farther away from Sioux Falls than mere miles would indicate.

It was his first trip to the cowtown capital of this state, his first meander up the eastern bluffs of the Missouri River, over the mottled gumbo hills that characterize central South Dakota.

At any minute, he expected to see a billboard of Rod Serling, presenting Pierre for our consideration.

Indeed, cruising alongside pickup trucks equipped with the obligatory gunrack, passing the great, gray governor's mansion where the grounds double as a refuge for hundreds of Canada geese, one wonders how the center of state democracy ever landed here.

(Consider, if you will: McDonald's Hamburgers does not have an outlet.)

On the other hand, where else could the capital of South Dakota be?

The answer, of course, lies in Pierre's location. It is equidistant from both ends of the state, far enough away from both the uppity urbanity of Sioux Falls and the hipster outposts of the Black Hills.

In other words, it is isolated from most distractions (save the Longbranch Saloon) that may tempt lawmakers away from their appointed mission. It is a place to work, to escape, to eat buffalo at The Bunkhouse.

Pierre is the smallest state capital in the United States, a city of 11,966 lounging in the shadow of the world's largest earthen dam, behind which Lake Oahe nurtures her mansized fish.

(That's a local legend, inspired since the fish are more or less held captive in the deep waters, feeding and finning their fish lives away and scaring the bejabbers out of scuba divers.)

Named after Fort Pierre, its dusty cousin founded by Pierre Choteau Jr. of the American Fur Company on the western side of the river, Pierre always will be a frontier town, despite early predictions that it would rise above its fate. Take the account kept by Ralph W. Wheelock as he and others toured several cities in 1883 to choose a capital:

"Pierre is a unique town, larger in her mind and in her hopes than in reality, but really having a glorious future, capital or no capital...Everything is platted here except the river bottom and that doesn't remain stationary long enough to give the surveyors a chance.

"Pierre had more of the characteristics of a frontier town than any point which was visited, but this is more than offset by a progressive business element and a refined society that will eventually redeem it of all rough features."

The history of how Pierre came to be capital is an off-told tale. Briefly, Sioux Falls claimed first honors as territorial capitol in 1858, then Yankton was chosen by President Abraham Lincoln because his wife's cousin had established a large trading post near that river town.

The capital remained there from 1861 to 1883 when it was moved to Bismarck, N.D. Furor arose in the south, but it wasn't until 1888 that a state constitution was drawn up for the southern half of the territory, naming Huron temporary capital of the temporary state.

South Dakota achieved statehood in 1889 and after much politicking, finagling and several elections, the capital was moved to Pierre in 1904 where it's remained since.

It isn't as if citizens didn't know what they were getting into. Pierre may have the reputation as being a sort of renegade outpost today, but it's nothing compared to its past.

In fact, one of the first things that came to light when grading for the new capitol building began was the skeleton of "Arkansas," an outlaw killed by the vigilantes in November of 1880 and identified by one of those same vigilantes who was still around, according to "Capitol Capsules."

Today, Pierre has risen above the reputation bestowed on it by border-hugging Dakotans. There are lovely neighborhoods with stately old homes, water recreation unparalleled in the state and walleye fishing that stands against the best.

The Capitol alone makes this city worthwhile, an oasis of marble and stained glass amid the sheet metal architecture. You have to wonder at the dedication and pride of the people of the early 1900s who saw fit to build this fantasy while contenting themselves with a spare existence.

Of course, a Capitol does not a social life make and some residents admit that barrooms and bowling make up most of Pierre's night life at this time of year. One, a young lawyer who grew up near Sioux Falls and had lived here for about a year, gladly accepted a new job in Rapid City, but will miss the people here.

"There's nothing like them," he says. "They're just so friendly."

Of course, there's nothing like Pierre at this time of year. While government is the life-blood of this town, the Legislature provides a fresh injection of red-blooded Americans, coursing through the veins of the economy like Grain Belt down a thirsty cowboy's throat.

The session will end soon, however, and Pierre will settle down to its normal existence as a seat of government, a stop on the puddle-jumper flight, a place to raise a family — and a little hell, if you'd like — with little chance of offending anyone.

It probably would just as soon keep its distance from Sioux Falls.

The strange case of the blue tiles

PIERRE, S.D. — The yarn sounded like it had all the ingredients: untold history, ethnic tradition, a tinge of mystery and a measure of fun.

They even threw in a Norwegian.

Yet, like most good yarns, this one has proven hard to nail down. There is no question that basis for it exists; state employees walk over it almost every day. Nor is there a lack of theories as to why 66 — or 64 or 88, depending on who you talk to — blue tiles are scattered throughout the floors of the Capitol.

Documented proof of any theory, however, seems nonexistent. Chuckles greet most inquiries and everyone knows of someone else who is supposed to have researched the mystery. And that person, who didn't really do any research, knows of someone else who did. Et cetera, et cetera.

Someone must know the story, though, and at a loss for more investigative reporting, this is a public plea to anyone who knows The Tale of the Blue Tiles. This is how it's unraveled so far:

The floor of the Capitol is a marvelous terrazzo creation, 30,000 square feet of marble chips set in cement and polished to a luminous gleam. It was laid in 1909 by Italian workmen who came to this cowtown smack in the middle of the Dakota prairie, imported along with the Italian marble that was cut into thousands of inch-square chips of yellow, rust, white, black, tan and green.

In the course of laying the yellow, rust, white, black, tan and green tiles, a bright blue tile was cemented in every few yards, in no apparent pattern, nor with any particular purpose.

Barely noticeable until someone points them out, the blue chips are scattered throughout the four floors of the Capitol. Wayne Whitney, whose custodial speciality is floor polishing, says there are 66 tiles. The tour guide says there are 64, while someone else is supposed to have counted 88.

Heightening the mystery was the discovery of several tiny turquoise chips, also laid seemingly without a pattern, yet special in that they're so unusual compared to the rest of the marble.

"I've spent hours and hours and hours looking for them," Whitney, a 13-year veteran of the janitorial corps, says.

Whitney says the Capitol tour guide for years had sworn there were only seven turquoise chips, but he found eight in the course of the last floor polishing, each of which he has duly X'd with a black marker to simplify relocating.

So here they are. But why are they here?

Well, Whitney says he heard that each of the Italian workmen brought a chip that they laid wherever they wanted as a sort of signature. One theory is that a single workman scattered them on a whim, foreseeing the toe-stubbing search he'd send visiting groups of children on once they heard the tale.

Pat Gerlach, a former state employee who looked into the tale, says she heard that a Norwegian workman brought the chips from his homeland as a sort of homage to this new Scandinavian frontier.

Dayton Canaday, director of the Robinson Museum here, knows the tale well but finds nothing in his records that explains the tiles.

The South Dakota Historical Collections gives a detailed account of the Capitol's history and architecture, yet the chips aren't mentioned.

Who knows? Maybe the workmen had some extra blue tiles and just threw them in, never giving a thought to the consternation they would cause in later years. Maybe they thought it'd be funny to jar the complementary patterns of yellow, rust, white, black, tan and green.

Or maybe the chips form some great cosmic pattern, spelling out the secret of better government.

Hence, the mystery.

(Photo by John Danicic Jr.)

SPRING

"When..."

The kite that got away

There's an odd sense of envy inspired by a headstrong kite.

And, for a kite flier of years ago, a sense of loss.

I speak not as a sage, for my age does not yet warrant that much respect, but it's always a bit disconcerting to find that the trappings of a childhood not yet a generation old have become outdated.

I speak, of course, of paper kites.

Few days were more momentous for a spring-addled child than the day the kite was bought. More than likely, it was picked up at the grocery store, along with the Fizzies and the Bosco. It came tightly wound around a stick, the paper crackling as we carefully unrolled it on the kitchen floor, a knee on the bottom point and a right elbow and left hand holding down the other corners.

The wooden sticks were spliced together and slipped into the appropriate kite notches — carefully so the paper wouldn't tear. There was a delicacy involved here, an operation on a flying machine that a child took as seriously as any test of the space shuttle. The margin for error was slim, for masking tape could do only so much.

Once the kite was assembled, the hunt for a tail began. Like most families, we had (still have) a special receptacle for rags, be it a drawer, hamper, basket or cupboard. Into the drawer we'd dive, seeking only the brightest cottony colors and lamenting the shreds of a pink dress outgrown long ago.

The satiny border of a small blanket brought back memories and allowed us kids to talk about "when we were little."

Once the rags were torn and tied to the kite, we were ready for the outdoors, running headlong into the wind and learning only after many attempts how fast to let out the string and how to pull and tug to salvage a tailspin. And how long it took to reel it in after it soared almost out of sight (we believed.)

It was almost inevitable, of course, that the kite would crash, and although the thin paper took the bounces surprisingly well, the time came when the rip turned into a hole and the wind blew through it like a fist through soap bubbles.

And we bought another one.

There is something about childhood that we're always seeking to relive, which is why I went in search of a kite the other day. A paper kite, preferably, perhaps one with Mighty Mouse painted on.

It was a fool's errand. Today's kites are not made of anything as provincial as paper. No, they're made instead of sheets of plastic and lengths of rip-stop nylon, like windbreakers on a string. Plastic tails come with kits that also include plastic sticks and plastic keels that are touted to have miraculous flying qualities.

These kites do not crackle, nor do they tear. They lie flat on the floor. They take crashes exceedingly well. This kite probably will last me forever.

In these inflation-ridden times of high unemployment and rising interest rates, I should consider it a bargain. Why, then am I slightly disappointed?

I'm disappointed simply because it's not as I remembered it, nothing more serious than that and certainly a circumstance that one should learn to live with. And I'll fly the kite because, paper or plastic, it still produces the same effect, that envy thing mentioned earlier.

Although the string is in your hands, the kite is the one having fun, skimming above the trees with all the effort of a cloud, playing dodge 'em with a sparrow, daring you to reel it in. The desire to shinny up the string and join its flight is fought only by reality.

Actually, it flies quite well.

Recipe for rhubarb wine: one cup of nostalgia . . .

It's that time of year again when spring is throwing off its jacket and running out to play in the sun, proud of what she produced in her short life and waiting to see what we'll do with it.

I like to think spring approves of what we do to her rhubarb.

In our family, we follow the dictum that if it's spring, it must be rhubarb wine time, a day of sharpened knives and painful amounts of sugar that, with patience, produces a liquid of no mean consequence.

Its main ingredient is rhubarb — one of the more misunderstood of Nature's bounty.

To many, it's little more than a weed, yet botanically, the *rheum rhaponticum* is a vegetable.

Some are afraid of it since its leaves are poisonous, while others dislike it because it is not to be munched without some preparation, preferably something to do with sugar.

Rhubarb is sour, the kind of sour you can feel back in your ears when you crunch down on a stalk. I'll never forget the devilish look on everyone's face when my cousins urged me, just a little girl at the time, to try the green stalk striped with pink.

My expression, I'm told, was everything they hoped it would be.

(I, too, have yet to be disappointed with the reaction when ever I pull the same stunt.)

Rhubarb also has acquired a rather negative connotation since it is slang for a heated discussion or argument. It's an association, I was surprised to learn after a cruise through the dictionary, that apparently came from the practice of early radio broadcasts repeating the word "rhubarb" to simulate crowd noises.

Whoever first thought of making wine from it deserves a medal for imagination. Or perhaps pity for reaching such a desperate point.

"The Recipe." Rhubarb in transformation — "something to look upon as your own." (Photo by John Danicic Jr.)

I grew up with rhubarb wine, getting little sips of the delicately pink concoction at Christmas, eventually graduating to thimblefuls and finally to the stage where I'm entrusted with a whole glass.

Making rhubarb wine is not difficult, nor is it expensive. At the risk of giving it the reputation of being cheap wine, it figures out to about 30 cents a bottle:

You start with rhubarb — lots of it — pulling each scarlet base out of the ground until your arms are so full that you trip over the dog for lack of vision.

The leaves are lopped off and the stalks washed clean of bugs and grass and other growing things.

Then you chop. We chopped 20 pounds of rhubarb last week, slicing the crisp stalks into bite-size chunks, then dumping them into an ordinary, that's right, an ordinary plastic garbage pail.

We follow what in moonshining country would be called "The Recipe," a set of instructions passed along by a late great aunt whose rhubarb wine was legendary and whose methods were foolproof. Ten precious pounds of sugar, or half the required amount, are dumped on top of the chopped rhubarb and 16 quarts of lukewarm water poured in. To that is added the juice of 12 lemons plus an unspecified amount of lemon peel. For color, she recommended adding some raspberries which we use in the form of two packages of the frozen variety.

That done, the can is covered and left to ferment for nine days, stirring once a day. The rest of the sugar, another 10 pounds, then is added and it's left to sit for nine more days, getting the daily swish.

After that, it's strained or siphoned into a big jug where it sits for six weeks before being transferred to bottles. Our jug has an air lock that makes for a wine of greater clarity, but my great aunt, using an older and simpler method, just strained it into her serving jugs and left the caps loose.

The wine is drinkable in three months, but is better if you can keep your hands off it for a year.

It's a sweet wine, better sipped by itself instead of served with a meal. It's a wine I associate with winter, since it's passable by Thanksgiving time, yet is quite refreshing when spritzed with a little club soda and iced in the summer.

More than that, though, it's tradition and something you can look upon as your own.

I'm sure that's how spring regards it, too.

The escalators of memory

It stood there, rising up from the scuffed tile floor strewn with plasterboard, the steep flight of stair-steps still gleaming like a ghostly specter of an old Ziegfeld Follies set.

That was Monday.

Today, those steps are powdered with the dust raised from the wrecking ball stubbornly jabbing away at the old J.C. Penney building downtown. Thus ends the saga of the only set of escalators in the state of South Dakota.

Moving the massive stairs proved impractical so, like some chrome captain in a gutted vessel, the escalators will go down with the building that for years was known by their presence.

The escalator store—I knew it by no other name, for what more should concern a six-year-old? Shopping trips that frayed even the stoic nerves of my mother were eased with the promise of a trip to the escalator store before returning home.

Six sets of escalators—three up, three down—towered within the core of the department store. They were a gimmick, and yet a necessity what with the amount of downtown shopping in those days.

"And boy, did they pull in the traffic," recalled W.E. "Gene" Snook, general manager of Carter Elevator Co., who helped install the Peelle Motorstairs.

It took six months to build them within the store, from October 1952 to the grand opening on March 19, 1953, a date Snook remembered with a grimace.

That weekend happened to coincide with the Class A basketball tournament that in those days was staged in the Coliseum Annex, just a few blocks to the north. Snook drew watch duty for that fateful first week of operation.

"Between games, all the kids would come and play on them," he said, noting that the nearest escalators in those days were in Omaha and Minneapolis. "They'd go up the down unit and down the up unit, ride on the handrails, ride up backwards."

Escalator riding was an acquired knack, for there was a fine rhythm required in stepping on the sliding stairs. Have you ever forgotten that moment of poised hesitation before you decided to take that first step?

Snook especially remembers a big lady—"I mean a really big lady"—who paused before she stepped onto the stair that by then was on its way up, lost her balance and began to fall backward. Snook supported her, grunting and groaning, until she stepped off at the top.

It cost about $180,000 to install the six units back in 1953; Snook said you couldn't get two for that amount today, a fact that discourages their installation unless a store does volume business.

Despite the seeming potential for accidents on the endless stairs, Snook said there never was a serious mishap. Heels were clipped off and scarves caught, but a safety mechanism that halted the machine if anything more than 1/16 of an inch thick got caught prevented any tragedies.

Unfortunately, that mechanism worked equally well when little 1/16-inch pebbles were tracked in, fouling the delicate calibration. In the end, it was the precise nature of the machine that sealed its fate.

"It just wasn't practical to move it because everything is so precise," Snook says.

"Besides, the state of the art has improved so much, and you've got to remember those stairs are 30 years old."

Indeed. Their unveiling came back in the days when dresses were $8.90 and men's gabardine slacks were $4.98 inside the four floors (and a basement) of the department store.

Photos of the grand opening showed men in narrow ties and women in then-fashionable boleros gripping the ribbed aluminum rails striped with bright emerald green.

Those old Peelle Motorstairs looked much the same on Monday. One could still remember the game of stolen glances and feigned aloofness played when the line of down-going people met the line of those upward-bound.

It became a challenge to try to step onto the moving stairs without looking down; we thought it was "cool" to ride up without succumbing to the handrail.

Only the arrows on the peeling linoleum floor directing you "DOWN TO 2" and "UP TO 4" reminded you that it had seen better times.

These days, the only effortless transportation available in Sioux Falls is out at Costello Terminal where a ramp ferries airplane passengers up to their loading points. It is not an escalator, however, but technically called a motorized walkway.

Escalators are by no means on the way out, although South Dakota currently is escalator-less. Sioux City, Iowa, has at least a dozen and Snook expects one to be installed here if any two-story stores are built at the shopping malls.

I hope so, for although I'm beyond my days of a six-year-old's simple appeasement, I still get cranky while I'm shopping and would welcome a diversion that takes me above the crowds of jostling consumers and into a world of fleeting fantasy.

"Mmm-mmm-mmm-mmmmm, is like a melody........"

When Hero turned villain

ELKTON, S.D. — The circus is coming to town this week, as good a time as any to revive the memory of Hero, the berserk elephant.

It's one of those tales that, like bootleg liquor, improves with age. Several versions of the event have circulated since May of 1916, when Hero went on his rampage in Elkton, S.D.

Some quibble over the number of bullets fired. Some say the elephant thundered past the Catholic church, while others swear it went by the Evangelical.

Bishop Lambert Hoch says he's got the unembellished truth, having watched the chase as a boy of 13. And if you can't trust a bishop, who can you trust?

The day dawned drizzly, too miserable to bring many people to the circus grounds of this town about 50 miles north of Sioux Falls.

The circus decided to pull up stakes and Hero was saddled in a harness that hooked each tent peg, pulling it up when the trainer jabbed the elephant's neck.

Now, Hero was a mixed blessing to this circus. He originally traveled with the Ringling Brothers, billed as the largest elephant in captivity. "But he manifested some bad characteristics," Hoch says, and was sold to the smaller circus.

He was quite an attraction, but his evil temper didn't diminish with the number of circus rings. On that rainy day in Elkton, jabbed one too many times by his trainer, he went berserk.

Hero went after the trainer, who dived under a nearby circus wagon, but the elephant merely nudged that over, sending the trainer under a railroad car for safety.

"He went right by these wagons of lions and tigers and if he would have tipped them over, we would've had a real good time up there," Hoch says with practiced understatement.

Hero turned down Main Street — past the Evangelical church, Hoch says — sending everyone scrambling indoors.

Main Street was a dirt path, with grass growing up to the sidewalks. Thus, it was not an uncommon sight for Ol'Man Swans to have his cow tethered there to graze.

"Well, this old man, he saw the elephant coming, picked up an old fencepost and stood alongside his cow. He was more senile than brave, I guess."

Whatever the motivation, Hero veered off and headed into the countryside.

Word traveled fast and soon everyone in Elkton had grabbed their guns — "everything from BB guns to high-powered deer rifles" — and had taken off in pursuit.

From 4:30 in the afternoon until well after midnight, the townspeople stalked the elephant, occasionally getting off a shot, but never fazing the pertinacious pachyderm. Finally, a shot generally attributed to Paul Hohnke sent Hero to his callused knees.

The fallen elephant proved an easy target and everyone got their potshot into the tough hide, aiming, Hoch recalls, "into the ears, the bottom and other apertures."

Hotelkeeper F.E. Gerlach, in a newspaper account, estimated that upwards of 100 people had participated in the hunt and 200 small-caliber bullets and 100 bullets from high-powered rifles were recovered from the body.

Hoch recalls the number of people out the next day, cutting hide for suitcases, and roasts for dinner.

How to completely dispose of that large an animal caused some perplexity until a college professor from South Dakota State University in nearby Brookings saw the value in acquiring the skeleton for study and made arrangements for his class to reduce the carcass to meat and bone.

"Equipped with cleavers, knives and a grindstone, the college professor and his class traveled to Elkton and to the field, and after some appraisal of the task, went to work," according to an account by Aubrey Sherwood published in Elkton's centennial newspaper.

"Hacking through the thinner skin along the belly, they cut holes through which fence wire was fastened, then run over the body and (attached) to long fence poles, which were used to pull the skin from the flesh, and the elephant was skinned.

"I can still remember (a student) coming up out of the elephant's body as out of a manhole, to get a breath of air and display one more organ from the vast insides."

The skeleton ended up at SDSU, where it was used in comparative anatomy courses and the rest of Hero ended up in the closets and stomachs of various citizens.

It was, perhaps, an appropriate end for the captive beast, to be killed while running free instead of buckling under the weight of age and an ill-tempered circus trainer.

Some claim it was the only wild elephant hunt in the United States; surely, it was South Dakota's only safari.

Certainly, the story still empties a few beers in Elkton.

"Who..."

Yakkin' with Gert

FLANDREAU, S.D. — There is a knack to passing the years and if you're patient, Gert Bidne will blab it to you.

First, you've got to quit smoking, no matter how much you suffer. Then get together with the gang around the kitchen table on Saturday nights and yak. Once a year, have a fling in Las Vegas (bring your boyfriend) and always take Wednesdays off.

And don't forget your morning coffee break. Close the store if you must.

At 83, Gert Bidne gives a jaunty credibility to that theory, having put 40 years into Bidne's Dress and Shoe Shop and not intending to retire until "the good Lord comes and gets me."

She's a reflection of her profession, stylish, trim and tall with painted nails on toes and fingers. She's hard of hearing, but plain-spoken, whether the conversation turns to diamonds or disabilities. In a voice that's always just a stitch shy of wry, she admits she's a fixture of this community about 40 miles north of Sioux Falls.

"I was born up over one of the stores here," she says, nodding toward the street lined with buildings of quartzite and clapboard. "My father came here in 1896 to set up a cobbling shop."

He died in 1939 and the business went through two brothers before it got to her. It was what she'd always wanted, but some changes were necessary, namely, closing out the men's shoes.

"You have to have a man to sell men's shoes," she says with an eye toward feminine propriety.

So since 1940, she's run a dress and shoe shop for women, these days catering to those in her age bracket, instead of to the prom gown set of her earlier years.

"Now," she says with an undercurrent of amusement, "I'm not with it."

Not much.

Three times a year, she goes to market in Minneapolis, accompanied by friend Lillian Eng: "She's my ears."

(This year's winter line, by the way, will feature brown, since she's had a lot of call for that along with big women's sizes. Also, red is always good: "I'll be buying red all the way to 44.")

Last year, she missed the fall show and her stock was sparse for the season, something that frankly was mortifying when you've been in town as long as she has.

It may have been just as well, though, for those flights to the city never fail to produce a well-meaning gentleman standing at the bottom of the plane ramp, hand extended toward what he sees as a frail, elderly woman.

"God, I just get raffy," she says, erupting before she thinks twice: "Of course, I guess I appreciate it, in a way."

Better those well-meaning gentlemen should see her when she flies to Nevada.

"I go to Las Vegas once a year with my boyfriend — I've got a boyfriend — we go to Las Vegas and gamble."

It's the perfect atmosphere in which she can flash her diamonds, heirlooms that she sports on each hand. There, she says, people just think they're paste.

Of course, she's equally as skeptical about bejeweled women back home: "The women who write their checks, pretty soon they've got their hands out, you know, and I say to myself, 'I wonder if that's real.' Dirty of me."

While Las Vegas is fun, she's most comfortable in her hometown, where customers are welcome to browse at the clothes on her window mannequins, Cynthia and Della, or just sit down and rest. That's what all the chairs are for.

She never thinks of her age, finding that the best medicine is to stay away from the doctor's office.

"You get some women in their 60s who come in here and carry on and carry on like it was their last day on earth. When I get to feeling what I call unnecessary, I just peel my clothes and crawl into bed. The next morning, everything's roses."

The cowbells over her door clang with customers and she motions that she'll be with them in just a minute. Meanwhile, they can look at what's new behind the curved glass of the old wooden counters or just get in out of Dakota's wind.

If they wait long enough, it may be time for coffee. And some yakkin'.

Originally published 5-8-81 as "Yakkin' with Gert Bidne, a Feminine Proprietor."

UPDATE: Gert Bidne is now in a nursing home.

Richard Cropp. "He had a definite military bearing that he retained all his life." (Photo courtesy Center for Western Studies.)

That duty business

Richard Cropp died April 12, 1980. It's a fact that hit me harder than I would have thought, for I didn't know the man.

Long ago, his friends said I should do a story on him—he was such a character—and I intended to do just that, always in the next couple of weeks. You know how that goes.

So when I read in the newspaper that he had died in the Hotel Park fire in Madison, S.D., I was shaken. Not because I lost out on a story, but because he had been alive just the day before. The fleeting, fickle fragility of life was laid out in stubbornly persistent typeface.

He had died, a friend said, while going back to warn two other women of the flames. But don't attach a lot of heroism to that.

He would have expected the same of you. Something to do with a sense of duty that I'll get to later.

Anyway, it became clear that a story still could be done about the gentleman whose speech was spiced with profanity and whose soul was smitten with Dakota.

It's a story of a person who loved birds so much that he'd lure cats into his yard and shoot them so they wouldn't harm his songsters.

It's the story of a man who left a sizable portion of his estate to a program dedicated to preserving the culture of the West, because he believed in that kind of thing.

It's the story of a man who drew a buffalo skull beneath his signature on everything he did, whether a casual letter or a finely-drawn map of early South Dakota.

Thus follows a recollection of Richard Cropp, a story crippled by circumstance, but made possible by memory of perhaps one of his best friends, Sven Froiland, a biology professor at Augustana College and director of the Center For Western Studies.

"He really was a crusty kind of guy," Froiland said, chuckling over memories to which his mind doesn't always give voice. "But he was very sensitive, too."

Cropp was born in Boulder, Colo., 76 years ago, and it was on that city's streets, he liked to say, that he became a historian.

"When I was a few months old," he wrote in a paper that survives him, "my mother was proudly pushing me down a street in Boulder when she had to pause for a funeral. It was that of Tom Horn, a famous gunfighter, lately hanged for his part in the Wyoming Johnson County War.

"This, of course, makes me an authority on Tom Horn and other Western History."

When six, he homesteaded with his mother and grandfather in Meade County, near where the town of Faith lies today. After a brief stay in Aurora, N.Y., he returned to South Dakota in 1912 and remained in Mitchell, S.D., through his high school years.

He returned to the East for his higher education at Columbia University of New York where he became the editor of *Jester*, the college humor magazine, a publication the dean thought "was ofttimes in bad taste." He was, of course, right.

It was customary, he wrote, for *Jester* editors to be thrown out of school and he upheld that tradition, returning to Mitchell just before the 1929 stock market crash.

For a time, he surveyed for the highway department, then joined the National Guard in 1936. In 1940, his regiment was called up to serve in World War II, and he fought in the Philippines until 1946. He returned as a hospital patient, but remained in the Guard for 34 years, retiring as a lieutenant colonel in 1961.

"He had a definite military bearing that he retained all his life," Froiland remembered. "And he had a twinkle in his eye. But he had a temper, too."

That temper, coupled with high standards, led him to leave his job as curator of the State Historical Museum in 1965 to join the Friends of the Middle Border Museum and, eventually, to leave his job as director of that in 1972.

"I think he sort of took pride in the fact he challenged things at that time," Froiland said. "He was an early 1960's student-type of guy.

"I've never, with the possible exception of Herb Krause, never met anyone with as much depth of knowledge. He had a tremendously large classical music collection, a gun collection, paintings, Indian artifacts. He was a photographer, a sculptor, a silversmith. He was a very colorful writer."

In fact, he was more than a little profane, prompting a story about a banquet at which he and fellow historian Reuben Goertz sat across from three ministers.

Cropp was unusually quiet throughout the dinner, puzzling Goertz, until the ministers left.

"Clergy?" Cropp asked Goertz. "Yes," came the reply.

"Well, (expletive with religious overtones deleted), I'm glad I kept my language clean."

Cropp, who earned his Master's Degree in history from the University of South Dakota, taught English for two years—"as long as I could stand it"—then joined the Department of

Public Instruction in Pierre, S.D., where he became assistant state historian.

By the by, he wrote the manual for school bus drivers; "a tour de force, as I had not ever been in a school bus."

During his directorship at the Friends of the Middle Border, the museum became the first in the area to receive national distinction from the Association for State and Local History.

"He was a dedicated Westerner who loved Dakota," Froiland says. "Plus, he had a healthy respect for the Indian people.

"This might give you a little insight in the guy: When his wife died about three years ago, it really shook him up. The next summer, he got sick and asked me to visit him in the hospital.

"He said, 'You know, I've learned I'm not immortal.' And asked me to help him draw up his will."

Another insight: Etched into the things he made—a black powder pistol, for instance—was his personal code: Death is light as a feather. Duty is heavy as a mountain.

"Duty came first and death, he wasn't worried about."

Cropp met death in the darkness of early morning. He was in Madison for the Dakota History Conference at which he was to present a paper. They all had been at a banquet Friday night and decided to meet for a nightcap.

Cropp, pleading weariness, went to his room. The others, staying at another place, were just barely in bed when the fire call came.

"We stood out there for six hours," Froiland recalls, "until they found his body. He'd come to Madison with three elderly lady friends of he and his wife's and later we found out he'd pounded on the door of one of them to warn her of the fire.

"She had to knock out a window with her shoes and climb down a ladder to get out and called for him to follow her, but he said he had to go check on the other two ladies.

"I guess everybody felt that's the way he would have wanted to go—real quickly and helping others. That duty business, you know."

Two rabbis and a nun

EGAN, S.D.—It produces the classic double-take.

There, amid the snowdrifts that linger in the ditches, in the face of a chill wind that whips the leafless trees, where the sideroads carry the muddy ruts of late winter, sits a fresh fruit stand.

You can't miss it. It's a splotch of orange oranges, red apples, purple eggplants and green watermelons against the drab landscape of early spring.

If that's not enough of a come-on, the sign advertising naked fish may help your foot find the brakes and bring you into the world of a man who doesn't know you're not supposed to have fresh fruit stands in South Dakota before the grass turns green.

Who is this guy, anyway?

"My name's Peter Paul, no Francis Peter, no let's see, Paul Peter Francis Malone—two rabbis and a nun," says the man in the well-worn cloth parka, teasing his customer.

He's run his little shop on Highway 34 just east of Egan for 10 years now, open year-round and supplied by produce trucked up from Mexico. The only trouble, he says, is keeping the heater running for the three or four months of the year it really gets cold so the fruits and vegetables don't spoil.

He's not always successful.

While the tangerines taste good and the grapefruit looks juicy, the eggplants are a bit suspect. Maybe they aren't a fast-selling item.

Malone doesn't seem to mind, though. Whether he sells or not, even the browsers supply an audience for his opinions, of which he voices many.

"The traffic? Oh, it's pretty good by here except it will probably fall off now with those idiots yammering on the radio every day how much gas costs."

The middle-aged Malone is a transplant, much to his apparent relief. He regards his Illinois background as a redeeming quality.

"Am I a South Dakotan? Deliver me. I'm from Skid Row, Chicago. Bought this place 10 years ago for the fish," he says, nodding in the general direction of Silver Lake. "Couldn't sell enough bullheads this year. I ran out a long time ago."

Which brings up the subject of naked fish.

"Well," he says, measuring you with squinted eye as to just how much you'll believe, "have you ever seen a fish come out of the water wearing overalls?"

Good point.

Malone's roadside domain also includes a Frigidaire stocked full of frozen trout from Lake Superior. Across the open garage, sacks of potatoes line the walls while a pile of cardboard boxes lie jumbled in the corner.

Golden bottles of cider and honey form a backdrop for the grapes, tangerines and watermelons on the rough plank table. Outside, potted plants bend in the stiff breeze.

Later in the year, the ground will be polka-dotted with pumpkins — "the only way to really make pie."

Malone, a paunchy, grizzled man who rolls his own cigarettes, enjoys the business that lets him set his own hours. And he enjoys the people who make his market a regular stop.

Martha Smith and Theodore Volby are two such steady customers who stop on their way from Madison to Pipestone where they shop for groceries.

"Paul always peels our oranges for us when we stop," Mrs. Smith says, grinning at Malone while refusing an offer of a second orange proffered without charge.

Volby, meanwhile, wryly observes with the common sense gained in his 91 years, that the business might be more profitable if the proprietor didn't give away so many free samples.

In short, the gruff, opinionated Malone is a soft touch.

"Well, I may not be here next year. You never know," Malone retorts, then mumbles sarcastically, "price of gas, you know."

A God-given talent

SIOUX CENTER, Iowa — When Evert Wandscheer was a kid, back in the 1890s, he rigged a dry-cell battery to a little box, sending it down a track to the end of the half-mile driveway.

When the mailman made his delivery, he'd trip the switch and send the box clattering back to the homestead.

Neat, huh?

It was only the beginning.

Wandscheer and his brothers then set about inventing the corn sheller, opening the door for "The Family of Celebrated Hummer-Spring Corn Shellers and Engines," as told in the dog-eared catalog on the living room table.

Today, parishioners at almost 200 area churches are kept warm by Wandscheer furnaces. The Iowa Highway Department uses Wandscheer snow scrapers that swing free when the road grader hits a concealed stump or rock. Farmers across the country use Wandscheer Heat Reclaimers and Ventilators in livestock sheds.

Wandscheer has earned more than 100 patents or patents pending in his 93 years. He could be a rich man, his neighbors say, had he not sold the manufacturing rights to many of his inventions.

It's only to be expected. Looking around his well-kept home on the manicured corner lot, a home cozy with family photos sitting on doily-covered tables, you get the feeling the money would just be a burden.

"It's a God-given talent," he says at each attempt to compliment him on his work. "I give God all the glory and praise. God reveals it to you."

Some of those revelations include constructing the first corn picker in the area, an invention the seven Wandscheer brothers made just for themselves, not bothering with a patent back in 1898. When they put together a corn sheller in 1910, however, they received a patent and manufactured the machines for years.

From there, Wandscheer invented a furnace, guaranteeing that if a cigarette paper discolored when placed over the vent, you wouldn't have to pay a cent.

"I never had to give one away, either," he says, his blue eyes reflecting pride behind his rimless bifocals. A thinning head of gray-white hair complements the dark gray of the suit he wears when company is coming. A hearing aid fills each ear after almost a century of listening.

"Those furnaces are all over the country today, like spots on a dog. Some of them have been running for 40 years. Quality and economy. That's what I always went for."

A few years ago, the Iowa Highway Department got wind of his talents and asked him to invent a contraption that would swing away from the regular snowplow when it hit an immovable object, instead of breaking the machine as in the past.

Hence, the patented breakaway shear pin that pops the scraper back when it hits a snow-covered stump, rock or mailbox.

They're useful items, these things that Wandscheer invents. But they're just the officially recognized legacy of a man who has been helping people all his life. In the course of conversation, he'll tell you how to get rid of the hiccups (soda and orange juice) or how to cure lockjaw (apply kerosene to the neck) or how to stop a wound from bleeding (place a silver coin over it; a rag leaks.)

"When I was in school, we didn't learn things like how to kick a ball. We learned what to do when a rattlesnake bites you, how to protect yourself."

Common sense things.

That, and a real concern for those less fortunate, has led the Dutchman to help others, like the clubfooted woman whose shoe he rebuilt to keep her toes from curling back.

Or the tricycle he made for a young girl with polio. "I told her she'd never learn to walk with those braces so I rigged her up a tricycle she could ride and strengthen those muscles. First, she just started out riding around the basement here, but pretty soon, she was riding all over."

Or the neighbor who cut the tendons of his foot in a farm accident. Wandscheer made a spring-loaded frame for the flopping foot that kept it tight to the body so the handicap is hardly noticeable.

These aren't inventions he's going to patent. These are just things he does because people need them. And because, he says, God has shown him how.

"You think about that, you know. My wife, Gertie, she died six years ago. Only my one sister still is living. I was born before this town was here. As you get to be my age, you long for the Eternal Home. It's something nice to look forward to."

Does he have any more brainstorms brewing? You bet.

"I've got two more ideas — how to make a lawn mower that will cut around trees and fenceposts and how to make a combine that will bind straw instead of just dropping it out the end.

"I know how to do it, too, but my son, he says, 'Aw, Dad, just let it go,' so I suppose I will," he shrugs.

Who knows? Maybe the grass needs mowing in heaven.

UPDATE: Evert Wandscheer died in 1983. His son Harold is still inventing.

"Looky, looky, here comes Cooky . . ."

BRANDON, S.D. — Ralph Cook stocks a marvelous freezer, bristling with opossum and catfish, snapping turtles and snakes.

Only once has a class been denied his hands-on style of educating, thwarted by the untimely thawing of a mistakenly pulled plug.

No doubt, he felt obliged to apologize since, to borrow a line from Ralph Cook's favorite book, "The secret of education lies in respecting the pupil."

At some point during his 22 years here, that line from Emerson probably has been strung across the blackboard in Cook's neat penmanship, an amoeba of thought amid the pickled pig fetuses and yellowing skeletons of his biology lab.

Those daily quotations from a worn copy of "The New Dictionary of Thoughts" are as much an indication of the man as they are an indicator for the students.

In a time when we're not only worried that Johnny can't write, but that Johnny's teacher can't either, it's nice to know that Ralph Cook has been teaching students with a commitment rarely matched these days.

"To me, he's just what a community thinks of and expects out of a teacher," says Jim Van Gerpen, who also teaches at Brandon Valley High School.

Cook is retiring now, after 35 years in the classroom. It is time to retire, he says with the same missionary zeal that characterizes his life, because he is in good health. Indeed, though he turns 65 this summer, his compact frame still is well-muscled from years of running, his color-blind eyes still crinkling with boyish humor.

These years, he says, should be enjoyed.

Ralph Cook. "The secret of education lies in respecting the pupil." (Photo by John Danicic Jr.)

("He whom God hath gifted with the love of retirement, possesses, as it were, an extra sense." Bulwer.)

He leaves behind students who revered his mind and dreaded his grades. He takes with him an old-school philosophy that's survived open classrooms and exploratory periods.

And he departs with some strong words for teachers and parents, a reaction born of his own unfortunate experiences with education and family.

"Looky, looky, here comes Cooky."

That goofy song lyric from the late 1930s tagged Cook while he was star two-miler at Dakota Wesleyan University in Mitchell, S.D. He loved it, because the nickname signaled his first real recognition in life.

Ralph Edward Cook was born south of Kimball, S.D., in a house homesteaded by his grandfather. He attended the same schoolhouse his father had attended, walking across the same pastures of central South Dakota.

Ironically, a teacher was his worst enemy as a child, a schoolmarm who boarded with them and began to ridicule Cook's reading in class. He developed a severe inferiority complex, only to later discover the poignant reason she made him stay after school: She was afraid to walk home alone.

It was a stigma that threatened to dog Cook's life were it not for the twist of another tragedy. A mare he had been forbidden to ride — "We called her Bird, because she could fly," — became too much of a temptation one night. Bird spooked and he was tossed into a barbed wire fence, ripping the ligaments in his leg. A doctor told him he'd never walk unless he exercised the muscle, and a painful running program began. It was a turning point, for Cook finished high school holding the record for the mile and caught the eye of the Dakota Wesleyan University coach who offered Cook a full scholarship.

"But father was completely opposed. I was going to farm and that was it."

The son stood his ground, though, and was graduated with a degree in biology and social science.

Cook taught a year at Olivet, S.D., then moved to Egan where he fell in love with the fourth grade teacher, Mardella

Christensen. The next year brought him a draft notice to serve as a medic in France, but love spanned the distance. Every day, except for two weeks when an old boyfriend took his last chance, they wrote to each other.

Cook only hints at the trauma of the war in which he earned a Bronze Star, merely saying that "when I came back, I wasn't gonna teach, just loaf around."

He credits Mardella with jarring him out of that post-war funk. He served a year as principal in Miller, S.D., then moved to Flandreau, S.D., where he taught at the public school and the Indian school, with a stint of selling Fuller brushes in between.

Justin Jones, who was school board chairman at the time, fondly recalls Cook's commitment to classroom discipline: "You know, the teachers that made you mind are the ones you remember and the ones you threw peanuts at are the ones you forget."

Cook arrived in Brandon in 1959, attracted by the well-equipped labs. Since then, he's taught biology, a zoology course he warns is college-level and coached the cross-country team. Always, his purpose has been to inspire by example, as runner Lee Magnuson remembers.

"He thought that the only way to coach is to set an example," Magnuson, who now lives in Pierre, S.D., says. "He was always out there running with us and he expected us to not keep late hours, so he didn't."

George Gulson, the junior high principal, has regarded Cook as an inspiration ever since they met in 1963.

"His life is just plain centered around his teaching. And he's one teacher who hasn't been affected by grade inflation; he's never reduced his standards for high marks."

Cook still lives an exemplary life, rising at 5:15 to run a two-mile loop around Brandon's borders. He arrives early at his office so he can read a bit from the Bible before class.

"You know, I never saw my father read from the Bible — all the responsibility for Christianity fell to my mother — but I made up my mind that when I had a family, there'd be Scripture read every morning at breakfast."

Their children are grown now, Duane working on computers with the Air National Guard in Minneapolis and Onalee preparing to enter the seminary for instruction in counseling. Their youngest, Marlys, represents yet another tragedy; she was murdered in 1978 while in Texas selling religious books door-to-door.

"The biggest blow of my life was when Marlys was killed," he says evenly. "But you get over these things. When you've had a rough life, you learn to deal with these things and you believe in the Lord."

It's testimony to the proven traditions for which Cook has stood and the efforts that earned him the award of Outstanding Biology Teacher in South Dakota in 1972.

"I've stuck with traditional biology. It's the basics they need, not turning five or six students loose in a corner to work on their own because they'll do everything but.

"That's what's happened to our educational system today. We've let the students get ahead of the teacher and they can't get them back. The pendulum has swung too far."

Teachers have allowed this, he says; they've forgotten the original mission of regarding teaching as a service to humanity. Now, extra pay is demanded for any extra effort and classrooms have turned into theaters for video equipment. Too little time is spent in preparation and teaching students how to study.

Tough words, yet Cook has earned the respect of his peers, perhaps because of his concern for them.

"It's always been kind of relaxing at the end of the day to stop in and see Mr. Cook and see what he's doing," teacher Naomi Fields says. "He's always liked to inform other teachers about things, whether it was watching chicks hatch or something he'd gotten in for dissection.

"And the nice thing was you could end up leaving there with a plant he'd started for you."

Cook has seen the school change since he arrived. Doors have been taken off lavatories and some lockers are padlocked. Kids are driving, drinking, smoking and spending more than ever before.

Neither do parents escape his admonitions. Too often, now, they side with their children instead of the teacher and the declining respect for authority can be traced to the home, he says.

Yet, "the student hasn't changed one bit since I started teaching, not one bit. It's society that's changed the poor child. Students today are better than ever because of all the evil things they have to buck."

That sentiment may come as a surprise to some students who think he's the toughest teacher around. Truth is, the strugglers probably occupy more of his time than the aces, for those are the ones he thinks about while planting his geraniums or perching before one of his sacred fishing holes.

(Those of you who thought he'd reveal his secret bait for catfish in this column can stop reading now. It's locked as tight as that 10-pounder is in his freezer.)

"As far as I'm concerned, the kids have always respected me and I love 'em for it," he says, thinking over these many years with their many students.

"When you get out of the hole yourself, it helps you understand these students. You love them more. It's better than if you had the glory road all the way."

UPDATE: Ralph Cook is enjoying his retirement in Brandon, S.D.

"What..."

Seeing through stone, cutting through glass

JASPER, Minn. — With a rhythm established between his hands and his mind, Dave Farrar strikes with his hammer, turns the stone, strikes, turns, strikes, then tosses the neatly squared chunks into a bin.

"Looks easy, doesn't it?" he says in the self-deprecating manner of the cutters here at the Jasper Stone Co. Minutes before, cutter Paul Steen joked that all it takes is a strong back and a weak mind.

Steen has been here 17 years; Farrar, since 1964 except when he left for three years "to do something easier." But he came back, likely because he is very good at what he does.

How long does it take to become a good stonecutter? Farrar stops and looks up.

"Some never do," he says, tossing another reddish-pink chunk into the bin and turning to pick up another piece. Strike, turn, strike, turn, toss.

There is a rough sort of art here in the quarries of this small town just east of the Minnesota-South Dakota border, an art that disdains the easy bite of a machine and relies on man wielding a small hand tool.

A lost art? That's a little dramatic, for it is being preserved largely through a family tradition of going to the quarries. More correctly, stonecutting is a skill that's becoming the property of an increasingly elite group of men.

Huge crews no longer are needed to cut block for the great stone buildings that characterize the towns and cities along the outcropping of Sioux quartzite that stretches north and east from Sioux Falls. Concrete and asphalt have replaced the paving blocks of a century ago.

No, today's stonecutters cut for industry, making blocks for grinding material and to line the tumbling drums that pulverize ores, salts, pottery materials and paint pigments.

Dave Farrar and tools of his trade. "It looks easy, doesn't it?" (ARGUS LEADER photo by John Danicic Jr., reprinted by permission.)

The Jasper quarry is one of only three remaining in the United States to produce for this need. Here, cutters hammer each block for a specific purpose, eyeballing each piece for a good fracture point. Other quarries blast masses of rock for road-paving and riprap, splintering it before sending it into the crusher.

For this reason, there is something of a delicate nature here amid the piled boulders and heavy hammers. After all, they remind you, they are working with glass.

They call it Adamant Silica. Adamant, meaning too hard to be broken, unyielding. Silica, a glassy mineral.

Together, they form quartzite, a hard metamorphic sandstone so firmly cemented that breakage occurs through the grains rather than between them. Indeed, when C.F. Lytle of Sioux City, Iowa, brought his stonecrusher with the 2-foot wide steel plunger to his newly acquired quarry, the plunger cracked when it hit the quartzite.

Yet despite its strength — it is impervious to acid and withstands 45,000 pounds of pressure — the right tap will break it as easily as a window.

"You gotta remember that it's 98 percent glass," superintendent Carlyle Johnson says. "That's why they use it in these grinding drums instead of steel. What wears off just mixes with the product."

Now 61, Johnson has been in the business since he was 15, starting at a quarry in Sacred Heart, Minn.; owned by his father and uncle. He was born in St. Cloud, Minn., where his grandfather owned a quarry. Today, his son, Curtis, works alongside him.

They are an example of the family tradition that operates here where many of the workers are father and son, brother and uncle. More specifically, the Johnsons are an example of the Swedish tradition of stonecutting, an art that came over with the immigrants who sought the stony landscape of their homeland.

"A guy we had here from Scotland probably explained it best. He said that wherever you grew up, what was there, you had to work with if you wanted a job. There's a lot of stone in Sweden, so maybe that's it."

The company manager used to go to Sweden to recruit skilled workers, but such recruiting became more difficult and an apprentice training program was set up a few years ago.

Today, the five cutters here all are under 40 years of age. The last native Swede, Dave Marsell, retired about a year ago.

The process of quarrying the stone has changed over the years, thanks to the introduction of cranes and front-end loaders, as well as the scientific discovery of Carborundum, an especially hard substance that makes the carbide drill bits.

It was developed in the course of trying to make a synthetic diamond, Johnson says, and was routed into industrial when they couldn't get it clear. At $40 a bit, it's good for about a hundred drill holes, one reason why the cost of quarrying has soared. Quartzite blocks go for $434 a ton these days, a ton being fewer than 100 5-by-8-inch blocks.

The process begins down in the quarry, a great hole where small cathedrals of unsound rock are left standing. Because the rock must be taken out in blocks, there is no dynamite blasting.

"We just want to bump it a little to get it out, you know what I mean?" Johnson says. "We use black powder, about the softest explosive you can get."

Fallen rock is taken out by crane and taken to splitters like Jay Eggerud who study the 3-and 4-foot chunks to determine the best place to split. Most often, it's along the white vein — "the slicker."

He traces a cutting pattern, then drills holes into the rock into which he places bolts and pins that, when struck with a sledgehammer, split the rock.

It's hard work, "but I kind of looked forward to it," Eggerud says of his decision to follow the course established by his father and both brothers of working in the neighborhood quarry.

After Eggerud does his work, the chunks are sent to cutters like Steen and Farrar who reduce them to different-sized blocks, the smaller blocks used as grinding media, the larger ones as lining material for grinding drums.

Jasper quartzite is shipped across the United States as well as exported. In Sioux Falls, it went into Washington High School and the old Post Office.

In Jasper, the quartzite went into everything.

"There's a lot more to it that it looks like, you know what I mean," Johnson says. "It looks like a lot of backbreaking work, but the whole job is a lot mental. You know, you have good days when things break well and bad days when nothing goes.

"But you get the dumb stuff in your blood, you know? I've tried different things, but I've always come back."

Johnson has worked every part of the operation at one time or another. Now superintendent — a job he says was wished on him — he spends most of his time dealing with the head office in Golden, Colo., but gets down in the quarry as often as he can.

He talks of the hard work that pays by the piece: "A cutter, he knows the minute you lay that hammer down, your income stops. You gotta be self-motivated."

He talks of the instinct that develops in the best of cutters, how they never look in fear of their thumbs, but at the place where chisel meets rock.

He talks of silicosis, a chronic lung disease caused by the continued inhalation of silicate dust. It's almost unavoidable in an operation where 6 1/2 tons of rock tumbled in the huge drum is reduced to 5 tons. The 1 1/2 tons that dissolves to dust is wet down and retrieved, yet some escapes.

It is a profession for strong backs and steel-toed shoes, a job for people who enjoy working with their hands, who wonder what's under that next layer of rock.

"Some days, you think you got it figured out and some days you don't," Johnson says. "You can't look through stone."

UPDATE: Carlyle Johnson is now retired from stonecutting, but Dave Farrar is still at it.

Know Your Neighbor Club

It began up on Breezy Point, during a time so tranquil that Ted Wilson remembers when a deer looked in the kitchen window.

Back then, there was some distance between neighbors. Sioux Falls, still bounded on the south by 26th Street, hadn't yet crawled up the face of the S. Minnesota Avenue hill, up where the deer roamed, up on Breezy Point.

People were settling the country-side then, coming in from Illinois and Iowa; the men eager to set up homesteads, the women eager to set up a community.

Dakota distances challenged the latter goal, but a determined social nature will not be denied. Thus, in 1911, Mrs. Frank Brown and Mrs. Rozell Newberry decided to start an afternoon club, "providing it would be pleasing to the neighbor ladies."

It was, and the Know Your Neighbor club was formed, or the KYN, as Wilson calls it. His mother was one of the first members; today, Wilson is one of the veterans of the club now reaching into its third generation of neighbors.

Whether a fourth generation will carry on the tradition is not assured. Times have changed since the deer roamed on Breezy Point.

The club has changed, too. No longer are its members actually neighbors, now spread across the entire city and into the countryside, but it's retained the original flavor, passed on to their children. Few new neighbors are invited to join. It is a club of tradition.

They used to gather for card parties and short programs and food, oh, the food. They would arrive on bobsled or buggy, depending on the season.

"No one had a car in those days unless you were uppity-uppity,"says Marilyn Granum, a third generation member. "I remember my mother telling me that.

"Mom and Dad, they'd come home and tell us the whole event and we'd sit around, us six kids, eating it up."

The club since has moved away from its original purpose of getting to know the family over the fenceline to becoming a service organization, donating time and trinkets to children's groups and retirement homes.

They still look after their own, though, serving wedding receptions and funerals, remembering birthdays and helping out during tragedies. They still have annual Christmas parties, picnics and "skip days" when they journey to Minnesota's Blue Mound, for instance.

Just last Saturday, they were all celebrating Nellie Iverson's 94th birthday, she having been a club member of long standing.

"It is a group I must say I have dearly loved," says this year's chairman, Geneva Grave. "Rarely do I come away with any ill feeling after we've met like I do at some things. You know sometimes how you can get all worked up?"

Indeed, it is a relaxed group, with two officers, two program planners and $2 dues from the 18 or so active families.

Those dues are stretched a little thin these days, since so many of the older members were ill this winter. The club also tends to stall a bit over the winter since so many members go south. Mrs. Grave has to punctuate her identification of fairly recent pictures with the disclaimer of who has died.

The future? Well, they hope to interest the fourth generation in continuing the club, although realizing that may be stymied. Not for lack of interest on their children's part, they're quick to point out, but for sheer inability.

Women are working away from home these days; many children are moving away from their hometowns. And time, well, who has enough of that?

"There's definitely the interest there," Mrs. Granum says firmly, "but with their jobs and their kids, it's hard to say."

Oh, they probably will. When you grow up with neighborliness, you tend to perpetuate it. And despite the social scientists' gloomy reports, people still take time to visit, even if the coffee is instant and the cream is artificial.

And Breezy Point has curbs and gutters.

UPDATE: The KYN club is still active, meeting every month, doing good works and celebrating special dates in the lives of the dozen or so families involved.

Fern Swanson at work. "If they knew how good this job is for your health, every woman in town would want my job." (ARGUS LEADER photo by Lloyd Cunningham, reprinted by permission.)

Hauling garbage, exuding dignity

It's obvious at once that the kitchen table is home base for Fern Swanson's family

The tablecloth of gold print fabric is slightly faded from the rubbing of elbows propped up over a page of homework. An Easter lily collecting late afternoon sunshine from the west window spikes through a hodgepodge of newspapers in varying stages of being read.

There is a positiveness among those seated here that is contagious. Wisecracks quickly are followed by affection. An afternoon snack appears from a crumpled bakery bag—snarfies, according to 16-year-old Gordy.

"Hmmm, I thought that's what we always called munchies," his mother says, once again on the catch-up end of the ever-changing high school jargon.

You can bet they'll be called snarfies from now on. That's the way this family works, the way they adjust to new things.

They can do this perhaps more easily than most because they have adjusted to a very major change in their lives—loss of a husband and father.

Warren Swanson died unexpectedly of heart failure last September just as he finished singing "Open My Eyes, Lord, I Want to See Jesus" at a Bible camp in Okoboji, Iowa. He was 45.

The Swansons had moved to their home on Route 2 a few miles east of Sioux Falls a year and a half ago, after the farm they rented near Dell Rapids sold for more than they could afford.

On the day of the sale, they found out about a garbage service that was up for grabs. They grabbed.

"Warren had always worked outdoors, had always owned his own business. This just seemed to be it." So in December 1977, Country Boy Sanitation began.

A photo of the Swansons on their first day of business is pasted among a collage of other pictures Mrs. Swanson assembled after her husband's death. In one, Swanson compared a string of fish with son Gordy's; in another, mugging with 11-year-old Catey.

"It was hard at first, putting this together, but then it became a challenge to live life like Warren did. Give the business up? No, at first I had thought of selling it, but Warren had worked hard on the farm, all the proceeds going into this. I could never give it up."

A sparkle suddenly replaces what has been a quiet, measured tone in her conversation.

"I've never been healthier either. If they knew how good this job is for your health, every woman in town would want my job."

It's tough work, with Mrs. Swanson, 41, and son Stuart, 21, getting out at 7 a.m. No earlier, Stuart says, "because it's important that our customers see us. And we don't like to wake people up."

The sight of a female garbage collector has startled some early risers, though. One in particular was the gentleman who glanced out his back door, then stared did a double-take.

"Oh, we have a person!"

She's made a few other concessions to her femininity, most obviously the fancy grillwork around the top of the truckbox. Less evident, but psychologically as satisfying, is the bottle of Wind Song perfume she keeps in the glove compartment for when she gets a ripe batch of critter litter.

They're usually finished about 2 p.m. but that's changing with people digging into their garages and lawns as spring arrives. By the way, Mrs. Swanson wearily makes one request of her customers: "Bagged and tied—please."

With a schedule of six days a week and a product that won't wait, maintenance is a constant concern.

"Stuart takes care of all that. He's stayed up half the night sometimes," Mrs. Swanson says with a mixture of gratitude and pride.

"Watch it, he'll get a big head," Gordy cracks. Nevertheless, the Swansons never have missed a day of service.

Being a garbologist, as her husband used to call it, is not something Mrs. Swanson intends to do forever. Right now, she's taking a course in salesmanship at the Community College.

"I think I have to consider alternative careers. I won't be a garbage tycoon all my life."

The laughter from this brunette comes easily and often. Dark-tinted glasses shadow eyes that keep glancing from child to child, joking with them, bragging them up.

"Margaret here, all 108 pounds of her, is as good as any garbage hauler in town."

"Better," Margaret states so matter-of-factly, with such assurance, that it doesn't seem a boast. With 22 (count 'em) days before she graduates from Brandon Valley High School, she's considering moving off the acreage but still will help out, splitting her time between garbage hauling and working at the Sioux Falls Care Center.

These are busy kids Warren Swanson raised—that Fern Swanson is raising.

"I always make my plans and ask the Lord to bless them," she says, crediting her church and a group of widowed people called THEOS for support after her husband's death.

"This just wasn't in the program."

But he's still in the script. Spoken of as if he was away visiting, the name Warren pops up often in the conversation.

"You should have known Warren," she says. "He had a common ground with everyone."

To which Margaret adds, "He could've given you a story."

He already has.

UPDATE: Here is the current status of the Swanson family: Fern is remarried and is a secretary, Stuart is a chemical salesman, Margaret is married with three children, Gordy is in government service in Washington, D.C., and Catey is in nurses training. They sold their garbage service.

"Where..."

Secrets of the blue wall

THE BLUE MOUND, Minn. — It rises as a dusky blue face grazing across the expanse of mud-brown fields soggy with spring rain.

Despite the modern-day distractions of fence rows and rock quarries, the Mound is as stark a landmark today as it was to the pioneers who first saw it lording over the prairie a few miles north of Luverne, Minn.

Shrouded in Indian lore, it retains its mystery even as cars whiz past on the highway below, their occupants intent on getting somewhere in a straight line, preferably paved.

The Mound has yet to divulge its secret of the rock wall almost hidden by bluestem prairie grass. That the grass is tall enough to hide anything is a tribute to what naturalists have done to breathe new life into what once was a burial ground.

"We're trying to restore it back to what it was before European man came in and how should I say it, goofed things up," says Robert Chance, naturalist for Blue Mound State Park. "I mean, we really messed some things up."

"We" is all of us — farmers who have plowed injudiciously, campers who have vacationed carelessly, snowmobilers who have driven errantly.

"The early settlers used to have to climb up on their horses to see where they were going, the grass was so high. Today, we've got some bluestem that reaches six feet. Back then, it was over eight feet, but we're getting there."

What those settlers atop their horses saw was a sheer cliff of blue rock buttressing a great upheaval of earth in the center of the flatland. Upon closer inspection, the bluish cast turned out to be the effect of light green lichen on the pink and purple granite. The name Blue Mound stuck.

Today, the southern face of the Mound is notched with an interpretive center, formerly the home of Siouxland author Frederick Manfred. A herd of buffalo graze on the northern end of the 1,450-acre park.

Some permanent residents of Blue Mound State Park size up a visitor. Buffalo may have been driven to their deaths off the wall of rock. (Photo by John Danicic Jr.)

In between the ground is splattered with rough outcroppings of rock. One jumble merits particular attention but must be pointed out by a familiar eye.

"These rocks line up in a wall like this for a quarter mile and they run exactly east to west. I mean, it is a perfect line. And it's very old, built even before the early pioneers.

"How do we know it's old? By the lichen. Lichen grows one inch in diameter every hundred years and these rocks are covered with it."

Possible theories are that the wall served as a retaining wall off which the buffalo were driven to their deaths or that the formation has some significance in the Dakotah Indian religion.

Facts stymie both theories. Excavations have failed to unearth any buffalo bones in the area and the Dakotah religion has a north-south emphasis.

Chance, however, replies that the bonepickers, the farmers who couldn't make a go of it, probably cleaned out the bones by selling them to Eastern companies for fertilizer.

"And as far as the north-south thing, we're going to try and check that out during the summer solstice. See that big rock up there? Well, if the sun lines up with that and the wall, well, we may have something."

Or if the wall can keep its secret, that's OK, too. "That way people can come and think of their own theories and maybe feel they've contributed a bit to the history."

Blue Mound is a park to participate in. You can squish through the waterlogged grass down by the creek to see a muskrat thread its way toward shore, hear the "kong-ka-ree" of the flashy red-winged blackbird or watch a spotted sandpiper make a strafing run across the surface of the lake.

The park is the only spot in Minnesota where the Blue Grosbeak nests. The rare Peregrine falcon has been sighted within its boundaries.

Chance is scheduling bird hikes at 8 a.m. each Saturday through the summer as well as a 10 a.m. hike across the Mound from the park headquarters on the north end to the interpretive center.

Hiking more than a mile by foot or driving four miles around the park by way of Highway 75 is the only way to get from one end of the park to another. A more efficient way of linking the two is creating some controversy. Some residents want the existing Manfred driveway maintained but engineers say the trail cannot be made safe for heavy vehicle traffic. Others, like Chance, favor a new road built circling the park around the east edge.

The Blue Mound remains aloof from these governmental and local quibblings. It knows it will outlive even those who are speaking about it. It probably will outlive such man-made things as roads, anyway.

A meadowlark lights atop a violet-shaded rock, its yellow throat quivering as it chortles its flute-like song. It's a sight that hasn't changed since the first settler rolled his wagon across the prairie.

You hardly even mind the airplane flying overhead.

UPDATE: Robert Chance reports that land has been added to Blue Mound State Park and that services and facilities have been expanded. Among other improvements is a new road to the visitor's center.

The uses of cobblestone

Why, a newcomer asked, are there cobblestone streets in this seemingly modern metropolis of Sioux Falls?

Are they merely a vestige of a time gone by, like an appendix of paving techniques? Or are they revered in some way, like a relic of past cultures? And if so honored, why do only a few patches remain?

It sounded like a story.

Turns out it wasn't such a mystery, after all. In fact, it was easier to track down than a muddy rabbit after a snowstorm. But that doesn't make it any less of a yarn.

(Well, judge for yourself.)

Ironically, the best-known patch of cobblestones is not indicative of early municipal paving practices, but of some enterprising private interest.

Anyone who has driven the length of 6th Street knows the place where the road nosedives with a tilt of San Franciscan proportions, or, depending on which way you're driving, soars heavenward toward the Cathedral.

There, for about a hundred feet, the smooth pavement turns into a rattling stretch of purplish stones, polished to a deep grapey color where the traffic flows and fading to a softer pink at the curbs. It's held together by sand tamped between the irregularly-shaped blocks of quartzite, a combination that's stood the test of time since the early 1900s.

The first method of paving streets was with a mixture of ash and gravel, "a mess," says Geoff Hunt, curator of the Old Courthouse Museum, who calls upon R.E. Bragstad's *Sioux Falls in Retrospect* as his source.

In 1888, Phillips Avenue from 5th to 12th Street was paved with blocks of stone quarried by men who earned 2 cents a block and averaged about \$4-\$4.50 a day, depending upon the strength of their biceps.

All told, 41 city blocks were paved with stone for \$2.13 per square yard. And, while an improvement over ashes, they took their own sort of toll.

"They were just hell on the iron-tired wagons," Hunt says. "By 1910, the automobile was pretty well established and their flimsy little wheels couldn't take the excitement."

Actually, the end came with the success of the big cement plant down in Yankton. In 1912, the first poured cement street was laid, that being improved upon in 1914 with the advent of reinforced cement.

Asphalt gained hands-down popularity in the 1930s.

Before the city turned to cement, though, some experimentation was done with creosoted wooden blocks laid on a concrete base on Phillips Avenue from 7th to 13th streets. The kicker was that they tended to float during a hard rain. They were quiet, though, and lasted 18 years before the creosote dried out and they were pulled up.

The end of stone streets also spelled the end of the quarrying industry in Sioux Falls, or more correctly, sealed the fate that had only been prolonged. The decision to pave streets with stone came at a time when the quarries were suffering from the depression of 1893, a time exceeded only by the Great Depression of the 1930s.

On top of it all, the Columbia Exposition in Chicago featured architects from New York who designed all the buildings in the gleaming white of the neo-Classical form.

"That's why all the buildings built after that time look like Greek temples," Hunt says, citing a building such as the Western Bank at 9th and Phillips. "A world's fair changed a nation's architecture."

No more was the heavy purple quartzite in vogue and, had not a street need been there, the quarries would have folded long ago. As it was, paving blocks were shipped to Omaha, Chicago and St. Louis before cement finally took over.

Thus, the best example of those days is the patch of cobblestones laid by John Randolph and Joe Kirby, owners of abutting property on 6th Street from Duluth Avenue east to the alley.

Cobblestone on Cathedral Hill. "The smooth pavement turns into a rattling stretch of purplish stones, polished to a deep grapey color where the traffic flows." (Photo by John Danicic Jr.)

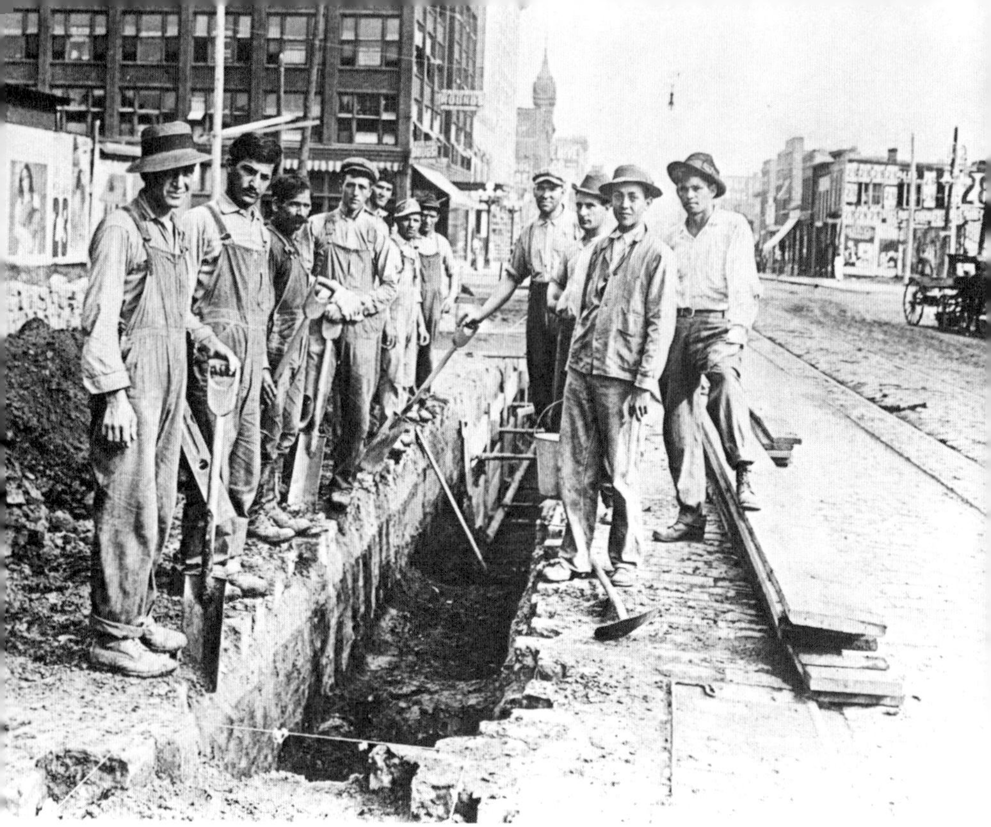

Laying trench through cobblestone in the early decades of the century. Streetcar tracks can be seen on the right. (Photo courtesy Siouxland Heritage Museums.)

There's also a stretch on the drive of the Falls Park and some stone peeks through the worn pavement of some downtown alleys.

But how did 6th Street avoid the asphalt onslaught?

"Well, as long as I've been here, there've been two reasons," says Ray Jorgenson, the city engineer. "One, if we'd ever get caught in a storm while they were out, we'd have quite a mess.

"And you can't wear them out. It's a durable, long-lasting surface and we've just never felt they were bad enough to be removed."

Besides, Jorgenson says, they're a reminder of our heritage.

And they're good for inspiring a newcomer's curiosity.

The oldest house — still a home

JEFFERSON, S.D.— There is a spindly little weed sticking out of mud slathered between the massive cottonwood logs that make up the 14-Mile House.

It's not a significant part of the old stagecoach stop. In fact, you have to squint to see it. But the dry, yellow weed imbedded in the ashen grey seam makes the mud seem more, well, muddy.

This is the real thing; not some plaster recreation of pioneer history for tourists. More than a century ago, this weed was growing along the banks of the Missouri River until Francis Reandeau plucked it along with a bucketful of mud to chink the cracks of he and his wife Dermatile's home.

That it still is there today is a testimony to endurance and to the care Francis and Fern Chicoine have taken to maintain this slice of Dakota history, generally regarded as the oldest home in South Dakota.

The 14-Mile House, so named for its distance from the river traffic center of Sioux City, was built as a stagecoach stop, store, tavern, restaurant and post office.

Today, it's home to the Chicoines (pronounced SHEE-quin) but they're used to people stopping in after reading the historical marker in the front yard or Boy Scout troops camping out back to fulfill a history project.

"It's a historical place, but we've put a lot of ourselves into it, too, so it's home," Mrs. Chicoine says. "It's really been a labor of love."

The Chicoines bought the home in 1964 and worked on it for a year before they could move in, stripping plaster off walls to expose the original timbers, rechinking the cracks and tearing up three layers of flooring worn paper-thin by the tromping of trappers, homesteaders and military platoons.

Located on what was called the Military Road between Sioux City and Fort Randall, the house today faces old Highway 77 about two miles northwest of Jefferson.

It doesn't look its nearly 120 years. Board siding put on to protect the not-so-hardy cottonwood from the elements disguises the log innards and still looks like new although the original slate gray color favored by Reandeau has been painted white.

Inside, walls have been added and the Chicoines have refinished the moldings around the foot-deep window sills and doorways. The original stairway also has been rebuilt with enough authenticity to fool one of those early travelers who returned to the place for a visit.

Miss D. May Miller was stranded by gumbo roads back in 1876, forcing her, her mother and father to stay in the inn with other guests she remembers as being rowdy and hard-drinking.

"She came back here when she was 105 years old," Mrs. Chicoine says. "She told us they had to sleep on pallets of some government-issue material filled with corn husks. Her father didn't sleep all night so he could watch over them."

The 14-Mile House no doubt was a pretty rough-and tumble place back in its heyday of the 1860s. Mrs. Chicoine points to where "a darling little stairway stood that we had to take out. They say a man was shot and killed there."

Men and women had separate sleeping quarters, the men upstairs where there was no heat, the women in the downstairs bar next to the stove.

The upstairs still looks as it did a century ago with the rough-hewn floor still delivering slivers and the Missouri mud chinking lending a dusty smell to the low-ceilinged loft. Mrs. Chicoine has a collection of lead shot pellets she has found between cracks in the floor even after 100 years.

As it changed the course of many things, the coming of the railroad in 1872 spelled the end of the 14-Mile House serving as a stopover point for stagecoaches.

It continued to serve as a post office, with the Chicoines possessing copies of several letters post-marked "Willow Post Office, Decota Territory, Cole County, 1866."

"This used to be Cole County until after the Civil War. I guess there were counties all over the country wanting to be called Union County after that war."

The Chicoines have stayed true to the home's history, furnishing it with antique furniture and reminiscences of pioneer days, including a shotgun hanging on the kitchen wall.

Oh, the television looks a little out of place next to the mud-chinked log wall and the electric stove holds wonders unknown to Dermatile Reandeau.

It doesn't take too much imagination, though, to conjure up images of buckskin britches and calico skirts, of gunfights over squatters' rights and letters posted telling of the new land.

That little weed has seen them all.

UPDATE: Fern Chicoine placed third in the amateur category of the South Dakota historical writing contest in Madison, S.D., in 1986. Her subject was the historical building that serves as her home.

A mighty oak — mighty old

BRANDON,S.D. — It was a sapling when Johann Sebastian Bach was in diapers, 60 years old by the time the first French explorers ventured into the Dakotas.

Settlers hunted with their new repeating rifles beneath the boughs of the 180-year-old tree. Thirty years later, they might have gathered under its wintry branches to piece together rumors of a massacre of Indians at Wounded Knee.

Today, it's said to be more than 300 years old — the proverbial great oak that from a little acorn grew — still keeping quiet watch over a stretch of river valley that Kim Raap has christened The Graveyard.

Raap is district manager at the 430-acre Big Sioux Recreation Area just west of Brandon, S.D., and maintains a strangely fatherly attitude toward the patriarch of the park.

He worries about building hiking trails too close, familiar with some people's brand of respect for nature. Better they should have to hike down into the humid river bottom and acquaint themselves with the sharp hello of a thistle.

Foresters believe the bur oak is the oldest and largest specimen of this native hardwood species in South Dakota, a fact that Raap agrees with, though he tends to humor a press release's estimate that the tree is into its third century.

How it came to survive the wooden appetite of homeless, barnless and bedless pioneers is a wonder. Perhaps its age — it was more than 200 years old at the time of statehood — was one reason.

Fittingly, it was already 128 by the time the chainsaw was invented.

Perhaps just the sight of it was enough to halt settlers eager to use the resources of the new land, yet reverent of its rugged beauty. Much like themselves, they must have thought.

The oak, with its great burls heaving in knots from the trunk, stands in the bottom of a grassy valley near a forgotten path of the meandering Big Sioux. Around it, naked sentinels of dead cottonwoods form an eerie backdrop for the oak's lush growth.

"We were canoeing down here one time and, I don't know, it just looked like a graveyard to me," Raap says, looking up into the mass of leaves. "Except for this one.

"Something that's unusual, especially in South Dakota, is that it never got any disease or insect. Think of the number of droughts it's gone through. Of course, the droughts alone don't kill a tree, but weaken it so diseases and insects can come in and finish it.

"Even for it to get started down here with all the floods that have come through is unusual."

The best estimates of foresters place its age at 300 years, based on measurements taken at the recreation area that lies about 10 miles east of Sioux Falls.

Forty feet tall, its trunk measures 11 feet 5 inches in circumference and its branches shade an 18-foot circle of gooseberry bushes and prairie flowers.

Several small sawmills operated along the Big Sioux in the late 1800s, producing lumber for local use. Indeed, many of the surrounding trees were felled long ago, with only a few elms, now dying from disease, left on the bottom.

"It's really funny it's still here," Raap says. "The cabin up at The Palisades (State Park) is made of oak, but the one down here was made of cottonwood. I guess it would have been kind of hard to get this one out of here."

Foresters say the oak is invaluable for wildlife habitat, providing nests, holes and whatever else is needed, as well as producing a valuable foodstuff in the form of its acorns.

A bur oak begins producing acorns when it is 35 years old, its production increasing over the years. Considering the two- or three-year interval between seed crops, the tree has produced an estimated 150,000 acorns to date.

The squirrels (forgive me) go nuts.

It's hard to say how many years are left within the deep ruts of the bark, but given a tree's average life of 100-150 years, there is little doubt that it is seeing its last seasons.

Then again, that's probably what some old fur trapper thought.

(Photo by John Danicic Jr.)

SUMMER

"When..."

The tents of summer

Tents, we called them in summer, those shelters we concocted to escape from view. Fort was a word reserved for winter, when great blocks of snow were grunted out of drifts and stacked high. The difference was important, for winter was a season which required a solid defense, while summer simply asked something to duck beneath every once in a while.

So each summer, with quilts and ropes and clothespins, we'd tramp to the grove and contrive our tents. They were awkward things, strung between tree trunks like captured butterflies, but they provided a sense of roof and walls and we were content.

I had forgotten this part of summer until recently when we were hiking in Wyoming and happened upon a grove of trees, with each tree spaced far enough from its neighbor that the grass grew to lanky lengths. The memory hit me, as suddenly and vividly as an old photograph slid before the bulb of a slide projector.

Flopping down on the pale green grass long since bent over by its own height, I was back in our grove, back in the tent, staring up at the small yarn knots that held the quilt batting in place.

Summers were wonderful in that grove. The trees grew in those familiar, even rows that distinguish a prairie tamed. On the outside were Russian olives, then some cottonwoods, then maybe five rows of ash. Each pair of rows created long alleys paved with grass. The grove ended with about 30 feet of evergreens, which constituted "the forest."

Quilts that I now would regard as heirlooms were entrusted to our fantasy. Mom would set her shoulders and decide that they were made to be used, but we nonetheless were told to be careful with them.

I don't really remember what sort of play we made in our tents. The forest, I know, had a clearing reserved for playing Indian, brushing away the pine cones until the ground was bare and building a campfire in the center. Or a place where a campfire would have been if the Great White Mother had let her children light one. We imagined our smoke signals.

A tent's possibilities, on the other hand, were so varied that no one memory survives. The game may have been nothing more complicated than going out and coming in. Maybe we brought our Barbie dolls into the wilds.

Sometimes, we would lay half-in, half-out and just watch the birds swoop through the treetops, listening to the crows caw their presence. Other times, Mom would coax us to the edge of the grove and we'd watch clouds, granting them identities, then others, then others as they shifted shapes. Then we'd scramble back into the tall grass for a treat — graham crackers or grapes or chocolate chip cookies.

We wouldn't spend all our time in the tents; a day held too many possibilities to limit ourselves to just one. We were always ready to take lunch to the men in the fields, carrying the picnic basket full of plates and glasses while Mom managed the hotdish carefully wrapped in newspaper. In early summer, the sound against the car's underside was of the squeak of long grass at the end of the field. As the season wore on, the sound grew rougher with the stubble of whatever was being harvested.

We would find some shade, either from a tree or just the car, and watch the men eat. Once, when it was just Dad to feed, we all walked down to the Split Rock where he had seen beavers building a dam. We were fascinated.

Then it was back home and up to the barn or maybe to the haystack out back. We'd end up in the tents at some point in the day, then it was suppertime. It seemed we'd always have to be reminded to dismantle our shelters and bring in the quilts. What if it should rain? — and besides, we had to learn to be responsible for our things.

The grove is pretty much overgrown by now. The trees grew to shield the sun and the grass began to wither. Some of the trees have died and fallen at stricken angles. Seedlings have filled the alleys, some growing into trees themselves. The symmetry is gone. The evergreens all had to be taken out one summer and the new ones seem far too puny to ever fill the space between them.

Those tents are a simple memory amid all the memories of summer. Now we go camping, pitching our ultra-lightweight nylon tent with its roof of no-see-um netting. We've pitched it in all sorts of places, in canyons, on mountains, in deserts, at lakeshores. But we've never pitched it in a grove of trees, sending our stakes through a cushion of grass. I suppose the idea seemed too ordinary, and there is something about growing up that makes us strive to avoid appearing ordinary.

Which, of course, flies in the face of what that Wyoming hike revealed, that such groves are rare and that they can, given the right memories, provoke some extraordinary feelings. It may be worth the search for a new tent site.

Sunday drivers

Our family took a drive through the countryside Sunday night, checking out the competition, cropwise.

Yes, OPEC be damned, we took a drive.

Some will call it a selfish use of gas. Guilty as charged, though there usually is some social purpose to our gallivanting. The tanks of friendship are more important to keep filled than our tanks of gas.

It had been a long time, though, since we took a drive for the fun of it. A couple of gallons of gas — OK, three — were burned to see nothing of more importance than how much hay so-and-so has, whether cattle numbers are down on this-or-that lot and if the new bridge over Split Rock Creek will suffice.

It was worth every Arabian drop.

We saw that velvetleaf has entwined itself in a field of soybeans on the riverbottom; we sympathized with the farmer who must battle that weed.

A new house is coming up in the draws northwest of Brandon; we speculated how the snow will blow across its driveway.

The evening scent of grass still warm from the day's sun drifted through the open window of our car; we smelled its growth.

Such expeditions were a staple of my childhood. With a meat-and-potato salad in our stomachs and a cool breeze held ransom until sundown, we'd pile into the car for a tour of the countryside.

Nor were we alone, judging from the number of cars cruising slowly enough past our house to keep the dust on the road and meadowlarks on the fenceposts.

That doesn't happen as often these days. Living on a road that's become a thoroughfare instead of everyone's long driveway, my folks have noticed a decided change in speedometers. People are driving with a goal in mind; rising fuel prices have pierced a hole in the gas tanks of meanderers.

"Our great thoughts stretched a country mile." (Photo by John Danicic Jr.)

That's too bad, for Sunday night, within the upholstered confines of dad's car, we talked without distraction from the telephone, without competition from the television.

We pondered Saturn and Venus and the rise of the new moon, glowing like a bleached rib against the skeletal configuration of stars. We saw a farmplace turned into a dead end by a swath of interstate and wondered at the number of houses for sale. A lot of people must want to move.

We gossiped. We monitored the sunset as it melted like butter on a golden pancake streaked with burst berries. Our great thoughts stretched a country mile.

We saw alfalfa fields beginning to bloom, the blue cast a sign of woody hay. We saw a patch of fog no larger than an exhalation caught in a curve of a slough. We chased a jackrabbit down the road and, in turn, were chased by a farmyard dog.

It was — there's no other word — nostalgic to relive those memories, to know that just because you've grown up doesn't mean you've outgrown certain things.

Yet it was different. Gas wasn't as precious in the 1960s, or at least no one told us it was. That was on our minds. Then again, perhaps we've realized our time together as a family is more precious than it was years ago. It's worth the higher price we paid.

The old soft sell

"And indeed, it seems as if Nature wrought with a magic brush when she painted the rugged Black Hills, tinted its trees and streams; its rocks and mountains with a golden aura that surrounds the region now and ever will."
South Dakota tourism brochure, circa 1930s.

The Greek writer, Aristophanes, once said high thoughts must have high language — sage counsel that the writers of early travel circulars apparently took to heart, producing some engaging results.

I'd hate to think our thoughts have fallen, but the language of the 1980s, well, it's changed.

I was fortunate enough recently to strike up a page-flipping acquaintance with some old travel brochures of the late 1920s and 1930s and their flowery, fledgling efforts at touting a new region.

They were earnest little pamphlets and sincere in their message, giving the impression of a carefully worded invitation rather than the brash come-on of today's circulars.

Part of that impression, no doubt, comes from the subject matter. The Hills still retained an element of unexplored romance back then. The attractions were natural: The Needles, the buffalo, the scenery. They didn't even have Mount Rushmore.

Now we've got Bear Country, The Flintstones Bedrock City, Reptile Gardens and Story Book Island. We've got paved roads and running water in the campgrounds. We've got Trout Haven.

Now some of this is good and worthy; some of it is bad. (A current brochure points out that the Hills contain 1.3 million acres of public land, most of which is open, unfortunately, to recreational snowmobiling.)

But the old brochures brought it all into focus. They reflected the era. One brochure served as a pioneering model in the art of color tinting, with the rocks of Sylvan Lake painted a fascinating shade of purple. A bit gaudy in itself, but oh, the language.

The Alex Johnson Hotel in Rapid City no longer is dubbed "The Wonder Hotel of The West," that distinction passing along with $1.50 rooms and a cadre of uniformed bellboys.

I don't think anyone still calls the Black Hills "The Switzerland of America."

Today's brochures have changed with the times. The verbiage, while still verbose, is less flowery. They tend to speak in terms of "a camera bug's paradise" and "some of the West's most unusual attractions."

The old brochures spoke of seeing "wild denizens along the highway." Today, we call them deer and antelope.

They used to say: "The rarer atmosphere and cool evening give a zest to living. The nights are cool and provide the proper temperature for a restful and energizing sleep."

Today, they say: "Necessary to sleep under blankets the year around."

Tourists used to be vacationists and Rapid City, now generally regarded as the gateway to the Hills, took on epic significance: "As Rome was built on seven hills, so Rapid City claims the distinction of being built at the apex of several valleys whose splendid scenery is diversified with fertile farm and grazing lands."

There was an unfortunate tendency back then to speak about "the early Red Man" and the "pale face." Service at the old Sylvan Lake Lodge's dining room was "furnished by cultured Indian girls representing 12 different tribes."

These days, we've risen to the specifics of calling them Lakota Sioux.

And they couldn't say enough about the Strato Bowl. Located southwest of Rapid City, the natural depression gained national attention when it was used for launching stratosphere balloons around 1935. It's barely mentioned in today's travel folders, a far cry from a booklet published in the late 1930s:

"Like Plymouth Rock, Jamestown and St. Augustine, the site of the Stratobowl in the Black Hills will become a monument marking the course of progress in American achievement, the mecca of thousands."

Whatever happened to such hyperbole? How come buses are no longer "splendidly appointed" but merely air-conditioned? Whatever happened to the "real cowboys" that helped dudes learn how to ride a horse?

Perhaps we have become too cynical, too jaded to believe that something as mundane as a bus can be splendidly appointed or that anyone still uses the word "denizen." Maybe tales of silver-tongued hucksters suckering some rube have cautioned us against such sensual assaults.

We may be smarter, but it sure isn't as much fun.

Of course, there is an obvious reason for the depleted supply of adjectives in travel folders these days: There simply is too much to describe, thus not enough room to waste type on petty details.

Or perhaps tourism officials have followed the example set by Calvin Coolidge, whose succinct summary of his 1927 vacation in the Black Hills provided fodder for the next several years of tourism promotion.

As one brochure put it, still charmingly florid in its attempt to convey a simple thought: "It is little wonder that President Coolidge bade a reluctant good-bye to this western fairyland. Even his sphinx-like silence blossomed into the eloquence of 'I am coming back,' a parting drawn from nearly every visitor to the Black Hills."

The celebrated Mr. Bill

William Frederick Cody killed, by his own reckoning, 4,280 buffalo in 17 months on the High Plains. That's about 250 a month, or more than eight every day.

He also had a traveling show billed, by his own reckoning, as "equaling, if not surpassing, the magnificence of massive magnitude at New York, London, Paris, Rome, Vienna, Berlin and Brussels."

Given that, I leave you to form your own opinion as to the veracity of his sharpshooting claims.

He was indeed a hunter, however, always seeking fame.

Cody, better known as Buffalo Bill, knew he was destined for greater fame than he could find on the farm near Davenport, Iowa, where he was born. While in his teens, he was a horse wrangler, luckless prospector and Pony Express rider.

At the age of 12, he shot his first Indian, one biography notes.

A year after he married at age 20, he hired out as a buffalo hunter, at which time he accomplished his legendary feat. He became a scout for the Union Army and served under Gen. George Custer during the Indian campaigns.

Widely-read dime novels about his exploits soon made him a household name. He became a famous man.

Why all this background, you might ask. Well, in the summer of 1896, when pioneers still were streaming into South Dakota, the celebrated Mr. Bill brought his Wild West Show and Congress of Rough Riders of the World to town, headlining the first Sioux Empire Fair in this region.

Called the Tri-State Fair, it was touted, by the sponsors' own reckoning, as "The Most Stupendous Aggregation of Exhibits, Sports and Attractions Ever Seen West of Chicago." Buffalo Bill, you see, while certainly the most famous, was not the only entertainment at this prairie extravaganza.

The warrior and the showman. Sitting Bull toured briefly with Buffalo Bill in the "Wild West Show and Congress of Rough Riders." (Photo courtesy Siouxland Heritage Museums.)

(In fact, there were some murmurs that Dr. Carver's diving horses put on a much better performance than the buckskin showman.)

No, this was a fair the likes of which the young town had never seen. There was Hazel Keyes, queen of the cloud land, who made daily balloon ascensions, then returned to earth in a dive during which "as one almost screams with horror," she threw out a parachute that gently floated her to safety.

For variety's sake, she also took cats, dogs, monkeys and other small animals with her, dumping them out one by one as she ascended. Yes, they had parachutes.

There were Powder Face and Cupid, the horses who dived from a 45-foot platform into a tank of water. There was the daily trotting match between two elk.

There was a 6-foot-high maze made of cloth that could hold 1,000 lost souls at one time.

But the real attraction was Buffalo Bill, described by one enthusiastic press agent as "the most gallant cavalier of all time is no mere buckskin hero, but a splendid specimen of a plucky and vigorous and skillful Anglo-Saxon who has emerged with honor from the most searching tests which can possibly be applied to man."

What that Anglo-Saxon brought here was a 500-man, 500-horse show that captured what seems to have been a racial fascination of the day with gauchos from Argentina, Cossacks from Russia, Bedouin Arabs from Africa and vaqueros from Mexico, as well as "real redskins, warriors who have terrorized our frontier states" — all billed as primitive peoples gathered to entertain the masses.

The patronizing tone of the copy of the posters is almost embarrassing to read: "All kinds, all colors, all tongues, all men fraternally mingling in the picturesque racial camp, all born hereditary princes of the saddle."

A typical show included a horse race, pitting one frat brother against another, and a whole slew of attacks: the Indians attacking the immigrant train, the Indians attacking the stage coach, the buffalo herd and, as a finale, the attack of the settlers' cabins.

The crowd, coming straight from Oriental hoochee-koochee dances on the far end of the fairgrounds, loved it.

It is tempting to want to condemn such prejudice, however naive; it is also wrong. At the risk of erring too far the other way and condescending to those people, there is something understandable in their fascination with unknown peoples.

Many of them had no real knowledge of other cultures; there were no *National Geographic*s, no *Life* magazines, no television documentaries. They were, for the most part, the products of white Anglo-Saxon Lutheran Scandinavian upbringing.

They were pioneers conditioned to horror stories of the Lakota, yet most had never seen one. Imagine, therefore, the impact of seeing 80 of them at once, seemingly controlled by an unctuous white man.

Of course, the same thing happens today. We are fascinated with the unknown, with the Dark Continents. We still are prejudiced against "real redskins." The trouble is, those excuses of 1896 are history; they will not vindicate the actions of today.

No, the Wild West show was a ticket to mystery and Cody capitalized on it. In fact, according to his contract, he took the lion's share of receipts with the result that there wasn't enough money for a fair in 1897, according to R.E. Bragstad's *Sioux Falls in Retrospect.*

While he was a shrewd showman, Cody did not prove a particularly astute businessman, losing his fortune in a series of unsuccessful speculative ventures. He died in 1917 and was buried in a tomb blasted from solid rock near Denver, Colo.

The Tri-State Fair? Well, that picked up again after a few years. The diving horses gave way to roller coaster rides and Annie Oakley has been replaced by Johnny Cash.

A sod-breakers' centennial

ALCESTER, S.D. — There is something about light at dusk, even if the sky is draped over the land like a damp gray blanket.

A red barn and a white house reflect the pale glow of an invisible sun as day passes imperceptibly into evening. A farmplace floats in a sea as green as dollar bills.

Oliver Thormodsgaard lingers outside. It's strange weather for July, but golly, he doesn't think his crops have ever looked this good. God willing, the plug will not be pulled on his sea of green. He's got debts to pay.

He must keep his land.

The Thormodsgaards have been on this land for 100 years, ever since grandfather Eric bought a homestead from an earlier immigrant. Their story represents a centennial of sorts for Dakota's white settlers, a breaking of the sod, the pounding of a fence post.

Their experience is not unique, yet may be more rare than we'd like to think. Blizzards, droughts and depressions have pulled farms out by the roots, sending them into the hands of another family, another bank.

Interest rates, land prices and market manipulation threaten today's farms with the same fate.

Thus, the Thormodsgaards see their perseverance as cause for celebration and, on Sunday, invited more than 150 friends and relatives to the homeplace to review the story of how they came to settle in the wide fertile valley between the Vermillion and Sioux rivers.

Briefly, Grandfather Eric and his family emigrated in 1881 to Canton, S.D., where other Thormodsgaards had come before. They spent their first night on the floor of the depot.

The Thormodsgaards: (L. to R.) Oliver, Fern and Lee. "Born, baptized and married in the same house." (ARGUS LEADER photo by John Danicic Jr., reprinted by permission.)

They lived in Fairview over the summer, in a log cabin now part of Madison's Prairie Village. They brought some cattle up "from Ioway" and in August, bought property north of Alcester and established their farm. Today, it spans a gravel road.

"I remember asking my dad why they built on either side of the road," Thormodsgaard says. "He said there was no thought given in those days that there'd ever be a road there."

Grandfather and grandmother later moved east a quarter-mile "and my dad, he batched here for a few years," before marrying and expanding the farm. His parents lived there until 1851, when they built a home in Alcester. Two years later, his mother died and his father moved back to the farm. Eventually, the widower went to a nursing home.

Thormodsgaard, who'd farmed the place since 1946, bought his parents' 180 acres, a half-section, in 1955.

Since then, he's expanded, buying another 120 acres in 1971. It's more than he needs — "I think a half section of land should be enough for anybody" — but he's considering his son, Lee, 33, who came back to the farm after a stint in school and the National Guard.

Lee, who rents "three pieces of ground" nearby, isn't looking at Year 2000 yet. Instead, he's looking at prices that have soared to $1,200 an acre — "the worst thing that's happened to the land," his father says — chemicals priced like fine wine and a marketplace in which he is powerless.

His father sympathizes. He recalls going to the bank to ask for $150 and talking himself down to $100 by the time he got to town. He wonders at those people who seem to have no fear of debt.

"Well, if you're in farming," Lee says, "you'd better not be too scared of it."

The elder Thormodsgaard, contrary to the corporate predictions, thinks the future holds a return to small farming. He thinks a depression will eliminate large landholders.

"Farms get bigger and the farmer needs bigger equipment and pretty soon he ends up working for the implement dealers," he says. An International Harvester man himself, he remembers the F-20 Farmall his father bought in the 1930s, thinking that was enough power for anyone.

He foresees growing different crops — "maybe for fuel."

Livestock? He got out of that after visiting his daughter in Arizona, where he saw the production potential of the huge, dry feedlots. Returning home to his cattle slipping in mud, "I saw it was going the way of the poke tree and got out."

Lee is prepared to move along with the changes. He foresees more one-trip farming, in which several jobs — plowing, planting, spraying — are done in one pass over the field to save fuel.

More importantly, he brings a commitment to the farm, surprising even himself.

"When I was in high school, I didn't know what I wanted to be. Does anybody? Then I thought I'd try this for a while, got into it, and haven't thought about doing anything else."

"It's an independent life, you know," his father says. "When I want to go into the house, it's my business. When I want to take a day off, it's my business."

Still, he must admit, a lot of the land isn't paid for; probably never will be, for it is the muddy collateral put up against the future, year after year.

Yet he has to smile at how times have changed: "I remember going to town one night and talking to a fella and I said, 'I bet I spent more money tonight than my parents ever spent on luxury.'"

Yes, Thormodsgaard is a successful farmer, a quality that's enabled him to live in the same house in which he was born, baptized and married.

He and his family celebrated in that house on Sunday, on the lawn shaded with trees his father planted, looking across the road where a steel addition extends the wooden barn. As with many old farmplaces, part of its history — the remnants of the Thormodsgaards' threshing machine — sits out back.

And the crops have never looked so good.

UPDATE: The Thormodsgaard family is still on the land it has occupied since before South Dakota was a state.

Two love letters —

It was a hot August night in Chicago, sticky with stagnant air that had drifted around the block one too many times.

He was just sitting there in his shorts, his letter said, when he thought of that girl in Sioux Falls and decided to write a love letter to his memories.

Two such letters crossed my desk recently, similar in their intent, but different in their approach. One letter was triggered by an event, another by a memory. One was philosophical, the other poignant.

One was written by a retired lawyer as he sat in the office of his newspaper of legal advertisements, the other by a former soldier who simply began: "I just sat here in my shorts and thought of that girl in Sioux Falls."

Both saw the city throught a clouded lens, a softened view of their pasts. The soldier remembered it as a sleepy town.

Perhaps that's why people reminisce, because the memories usually are good and the sorrows are safely distant.

Whatever the reason, they provide a thoughtful look at Sioux Falls and the people who paused here for a while.

The first letter was postmarked Long Beach, Calif., a community that is called Little Iowa because of all the retirees from the Midwest. This retiree, Blaine Nels Simons, lived in Sioux Falls from 1923 to 1943 and returned this summer for the Washington High School class reunion.

He was impressed with his old hometown, he wrote, and was pleased that it is progressing in an orderly manner. And he was straightforward about his retrospective inclination.

"The winds of nostalgia are sweeping the country. They whisper across the farmland, they sing through city streets. Everyone seems touched by these mystic zephyrs of the past."

For him, nostalgia was personified by the class reunion. No one noticed the gray hair or the thickened middle or the crepey neck. They remembered themselves as they once were.

"My fifth grade sweetheart still carried the innocence of face that she had when we shared lunch together on the schoolhouse steps. A boy considered 'not too likely to succeed' was a multimillionaire. The 'most likely to succeed' was a top-level banker."

Sioux Falls, of course, had changed. The Big Sioux River with its bike trails was a vast improvement over the tangle-banked course of his day. Simons obviously was tickled about his return to the city and just wanted everyone else to know how nice he thought it was. His motivating force was easily understood.

The second letter was a bit more complicated, much more romantic and provided a glimpse into what life here might have been like during the years of World War II when Sioux Falls was an Air Force base.

Postmarked in Chicago, the letter came with its own title, "A Love Letter to Sioux Falls." It was written by a man stationed at the base in 1942 for radio and mechanical training. Because romance does not always linger in the hearts of both parties, and because metropolitan Sioux Falls still is a small town, he shall remain nameless. "Leaving Chicago for Sioux Falls was a bit shattering," he wrote. "I was a sophisticated 23-year-old Chicagoan college grad and suddenly I was in deep water with these unsophisticated but oh! so friendly people."

He wrote of the dinner invitations after Sunday Mass, the weekends of pheasant hunting and the mythical patrol that Sioux Falls residents had set up between the base and the city so that the servicemen never walked more than a block before a ride came along.

"They were all proud to be friends with us dumb recruits. Made us feel important, liked, loved, wanted, even idolized."

His letter was more than a thank-you to the city, though. There was, as there is in all good soldier memories, a girl. Not just any girl, he wrote, and certainly not one who would be interested in a private like himself.

"If my opinion had been sought, I'd have qualified her as a 'Captain' type at least. Maybe 'Major.' She took me home, introduced me to her Dad as the man she was to marry. I stood there with my mouth open — but he didn't. He grabbed my hand, crushed it and my shoulder with the other arm and laughed and said something like 'great.' I gathered this little lady was the end of the world for him and she was turning his jump rope."

Dad, he wrote, figured it would be only three months before the servicemen were transferred, so he just kept going to mass and praying.

And so it went. The soldier was transferred, and while they kept up a correspondence for some time, he and the girl never married. All the letters he'd saved were lost in a fire. Today, he has seven children and his memories.

"It's now nearly forty years past, but fresh in my heart is the memory of a great love for a wonderful Sioux Falls lady. Was she with the Telephone Co. or the Power & Light Co.?"

— And one reply

On Sept. 17, this column reprinted part of a letter from a man who once was stationed here as a soldier when Sioux Falls was a training base during World War II.

It was a love letter, he said, to his memories of a friendly town and — especially — of a special girl whom time had blurred. It was reprinted here for what it was worth, for someone else to recall and forget.

Therefore, it came as a surprise when the handsome woman walked across the newsroom last week, letter in hand, wishing to reply to that soldier in Chicago who sat up one night in his shorts "and thought of that girl in Sioux Falls."

She used to go to USO dances here, she said, and that letter reminded her of those buoyant days.

"Even the plainest Jane could get some attention. It was no matter whether you were fat or thin or not so pretty. All those boys were so polite that some girls just bloomed while they were here."

So it was that when she read the letter, she was compelled to write a reply. "Just sign it Sioux Falls Sue or something," she said.

OK.

"Dear soldier boy from Chicago,

"I remembered you well. I had often wondered what happened to you, too. I especially remember your buddy, Joe. Now he was a charmer. He was from Mississippi.

"One evening he sang to me 'Lady Be Good.' I wasn't exactly Miss Sioux Falls, but he made me feel like a queen. And then one of you fellas spoiled it all by saying, 'I hear you had a letter from your wife, Joe.'

"Joe blushed.

"'Joe, how could you?' I asked. 'Waal darlin', you wouldn't have given me a second look if I told you I was married.'

"Remember?

"After you and Joe shipped out, there were other soldiers, many more. We telephone operators loved the USO dances. Sometimes we took long walks. No one had cars, remember?

"Sometimes we invited soldiers over for Sunday dinner. You appreciated our hospitality, but we appreciated you and your buddies. Most of us had relatives in the service. You reminded us of them. We didn't do all the giving. You gave us something, too.

"I married the local boy I had been writing to. That was 37 years ago. But sometimes I remember Joe and how he sang to me."

"Who..."

Grandma

It was my arches that granted me my first insight into the heritage of generations. It must have been the nylon insoles of some tennis shoes, or maybe it was a pair of socks — this was a long time ago — that made tiny bumps break out on my arches. They itched. Then they cracked. They looked weird and I felt cursed.

Then my mom said, quite offhand, that it really may not be so unexpected given that Grandma sometimes had the same trouble with her feet. In other words, it ran in the family.

Suddenly, my plight didn't seem so bad. Perversely, it even took on some importance. This was not a personal tragedy, but one of those things that a family has to deal with, that maybe even brings it closer together. I had always loved Grandma, so having feet like hers made me proud. This was my heritage, passed down through generations.

I'm not sure how Grandma will feel about my talking about her feet. Puzzled, probably. Likely, she can't imagine why I'm writing about her at all. "Couldn't you find someone more interesting to write about?" she'll say. Maybe that comes from being raised Scandinavian, or raised a woman. Whatever, she's always brushed off any intimation that she's of some worth. We try to get her to record her memories of early Brandon, explaining that her contribution is important to its history, and she laughs and shakes her head, "Oh, what would I have to say?"

Maybe something like this.

She was born in 1896, and turned 90 last October. Nobody believed she was that old, mostly because she moves so fast, although partly because she still uses a slight reddish tint in her hair. She's always been known for her energy. Telling her to stay put is as fruitless as telling the Sioux to stop flowing.

Mrs. William Ode, 'Grandma." "She quilts like a demon these days." (Photo by John Danicic Jr.)

She quilts like a demon these days, and we can always count on a new set of embroidered dishtowels each Christmas, where they sit beneath a tree that holds lacy ornaments that she's tatted. She usually has someone over for Sunday dinner and is always going somewhere for coffee on weekdays. She's been caught mowing her lawn on the hottest days of the summer and shoveling her walk before the snow has stopped falling. She's got wonderful neighbors who are only too glad to help, but her idea of when help is needed often is about two steps beyond theirs.

I don't want to say Grandma doesn't act her age, because I dearly want to believe that's how 90 acts. Which must mean that the rest of my life will be a gradual process of coming up to speed.

She's always been that way. She helped Grandpa build up the farm, milked cows, did chores, kept house. It was steady, hard work and now it seems that's all she knows. Once, for a term paper, I asked them about the Depression. Their story was not a harsh one — people on the farm had food, and the dust didn't blow quite so bad as elsewhere — and inside, I was disappointed at the lack of drama.

Instead, they talked about daily life, of hanging chunks of slaughtered beef in the well to stay cool, don't mind the flies, of building rock walls and planting trees. It sounded like hard work to me, but they talked about it all as a matter of course. Finally, I caught on. They were working together, in partnership, which soothed the aches, whether of the bank account or the back.

Even as a kid, I knew they were in love, probably because he still teased her. I remember Grandpa's actions more than hers, but that's the way it's always been. For her 90th birthday, all us grandkids got together to brainstorm some sort of tribute at the open house in the church basement. Most of our memories, however, were about Grandpa: his pockets full of butterscotch candy, or his almost genteel use of the spittoon. We girls were astonished when the boy cousins revealed some ribald things Grandpa had said in the fields — astonished and reduced to giggles.

As the evening wore on and we tried to recall some wildly colorful anecdotes, we realized for the first time that Grandma always had been a supporting player. Our memories of her seemed mundane: Wednesday night supper between school and confirmation class, watermelon pickles sweetly translucent, her "Var sa god" that still brings us to the table. It caught me off guard. Broken into parts, she seemed so ordinary, yet she was such a vital presence in our lives. How did this work?

Grandma, I see now, is the sum of her parts. I feel close to her not because her arches sometimes itched, but for a multitude of reasons, everything from her piles of photo albums, to her livingroom picture of a young girl in a long gown, to her kiss hello at the front door. It all blends together, like cookie batter.

It's a fact of life that cookie batter tastes best right out of the bowl, just mixed, its ingredients still tasting of themselves, not yet transformed by baking. It's still in its elemental state, and that is how I think of Grandma. Her values of family (love it), money (save it), and work (do it) are basic and worthy. She is as much a recipe for life as the one she enclosed with her wedding gift to us. It sounds a little corny, but makes a lot of sense:

4 cups love, 2 cups loyalty, 3 cups forgiveness, 1 cup friendship, 5 spoons of hope, 2 spoons of tenderness, 4 qts. faith, 1 barrel of laughter. Bake it with sunshine. Serve daily in generous helpings.

The Road to Woolies

SALEM, S.D. — They should be in a road picture: Leith and Kearin on the Road to Suffolk.

Their rapid-fire dialogue, spliced with one-liners, is reminiscent of the quips once traded between Bob Hope and Bing Crosby. The situations they get themselves into rival the slapstick comedy of any team.

But Dick Leith and Sid Kearin aren't thumbing their way from Morocco to Rio to Zanzibar. More like Salem to Madison to Watertown. And they aren't fighting over the girl, although they may be accused of making sheep's eyes.

Leith and Kearin, you see, are sheep shearers by trade, friends by choice and a comedy team by default.

"We been together oh, 15, 20 years now," Leith says. "Course, we haven't worked every job together. I don't get along with him that well."

They manage, though, defrocking the bleeting bundles of wool with amazing ease despite the 300 pounds of feisty mutton struggling beneath the clippers at the John Eichacker farm south of Salem.

Kearin ("How do you spell that?" "Same way my father did.") is the junior partner at 59, "and I'm still pretty damn good-looking." He started shearing when he was 14 years old, shaving sheep by blade for 10 cents a head.

"You have to take a course in religion, too, before you start 'cuz you swear so much," he added, his brown eyes shining in an angular, deadpan face.

"Back in the Thirties, there was nothing else to do," Leith, 62, says of his initiation. "Two guys came up to me back in '38 and said they needed somebody to catch sheep so I did it for $1.25 a day plus lodging. They didn't tell me they were 10-hour days. After we got out West where they couldn't find anybody else, I asked for $1.50."

With his graying hair held back by a red bandanna, Leith looks like South Dakota's version of singer Willie Nelson. He sheared for John Morrell & Co. during World War II and at Ellis, S.D., when the feedlot there used to hold 35,000 sheep.

"You used to have to fight for sheep back then, a real cut-throat business. Sheared for 15 cents a head. If I had a nickel for every head I've sheared, I'd leave my machine and everything right here. Just take my clothes."

"Hell, I'd go home naked," Kearin quips.

The two got together about 15 years ago. "He needed help," Leith says, his attempt at sounding put-upon betrayed by a grin. "We'd heard of each other for some time and just got together," adds Kearin, taking the ribbing in stride.

Today, they say, there are no young shearers; all the practitioners now are their age and older, citing a Centerville man who still shears at age 75. "Yeah, but he needs the money," Leith says, chuckling.

"No one wants to do this dirty job. The sheep here aren't so bad, but get 'em after they've been out in the pasture or in the mud — you might as well roll in it before you start 'cuz you'll have it all over you.

"For a kid who wants to learn, it could put him through school."

"Course you smell pretty bad, too," Kearin adds.

"Smells like money," Leith retorts, nose wrinkling.

Leith, of Roswell, S.D., and Kearin, Madison, S.D., shear ewes for $1.50 a head and lambs for $1.25. "Geez, don't put that down or we'll have the Internal Revenue Service down on us in a minute," Kearin says, feigning fear.

"Either that, or have every farmer in the country calling us with a job," Leith rejoins, leaving you to wonder if that's an exceptionally high or low rate.

Kearin plans on answering fewer of those phone calls now. After 42 years of shearing, he's thinking about unplugging the clippers, "Not too long after this year," he says.

"Aw, come on, seems like I've heard that for the last 20 years," Leith kids.

"No, not too long after this year," Kearin repeats, not picking up on the humor. His shoulders are broad despite his slight build, strengthened from hogtying up to 100 sheep on a good day.

Kearin's best day? Back some time ago when he went through 160 lambs.

"Whew, you musta needed the money," Leith says, shaking his head.

The two men jab out their cigarettes and prepare to tackle their woolly foes once again. Those conquered run around the yard, looking as if they're wearing long underwear. Those under the clippers wear little more than a mortified look.

The wool falls off in sections, like a peel from an orange, to be packed while still warm from the body into huge burlap sacks.

"Need some help over there?" Leith asks his partner grappling with a 300-pound buck.

"No thanks," Kearin puffs in reply.

"Heck, I thought if I helped you with yours, you'd help me with mine," Leith grumbles, then grins as he wrestles another ewe to the ground.

Wonder what Dorothy Lamour would look like in sheepskin?

UPDATE: Dick Leith has retired from shearing, but Sid Kearin is still active on the job he has been working at for over 50 years.

Doing something about the weather

JORDAN, Minn. — It might not be the first question we ask each morning, but it's right up there with "Omigod, did I oversleep?" Once that one is answered, curiosity turns to how hot (or cold) it's going to get today, or whether it's going to rain (or snow).

These statistics affect what we wear, what we pack in our lunch, whether we drive or take the bus. Perhaps most important, they establish our mood for the day. Who knows? Someday a social anthropologist (with skill for grant-writing) may correlate great events in history with the particular weather conditions. Maybe Gen. William Tecumseh Sherman, as he approached Atlanta, simply couldn't face another day of humidity.

Maybe not, but at least the raw material for such a study would be there, thanks to the dutiful efforts of people such as Mattilda Slavicek. She is one of 36 weather observers recently honored by the National Climatic Data Center for her 20 years of making daily temperature and precipitation readings. Each day at 6 p.m., she has walked from her white clapboard house on a farm south of Jordan to what looks like a giant birdhouse in the yard. Inside are two thermometers that record the day's high and the night's low. If it's rained, she measures the depth of water collected in the nearby cylinder; if it's snowed, she first brings the accumulation into the house to melt. Each month, she mails her readings to the National Weather Service, which uses them, and the data collected by 12,000 other rural weather observers, to supplement data from its 300 urban stations.

Slavicek is following the lead set by her late husband, Gustav, who died 21 years ago at age 76, in the house he built, on the farm where he was born.

"He'd watched the weather on his own at first, kept track of the stars and the moon and all that," Slavicek said. "When

the government asked him to do it, he was happy to, since it was right down his line." When he died in 1965, she took over the weather duties, although because she's 88, her son Robert spells her when the weather is bad or her heart is acting up.

She does it for the same pay her husband received: gratis.

"Well, I used to get a Christmas card," she said. "Now," her daughter Doris Kipka added, "you just get a friendly thank you once a year" when a man from the weather service comes to check the instruments.

"He might give me a pencil, too," Slavicek said. Her smile is wry, but it's all in good fun.

While a farmer can easily regard the weather as an enemy as well as a friend, Gustav Slavicek's relationship with the elements softened his family's feelings about them. "I remember, we'd all sit on the porch and he'd explain all the different kinds of clouds," Kipka said. "I think that's one reason all of us can watch storms without being scared."

For her two decades of service, Slavicek received the John Campanius Holm Award. Holm was a Lutheran minister who began the New World's first systematic weather observations in 1644. She doesn't think too much about being part of such a legacy, but the records she and others keep "are invaluable for finding out what's going on in this country," said Frank Quinlan, director of the data center's climatological analysis division in Asheville, N.C.

Slavicek grew up not far from Jordan, graduating from eighth grade in Old Helena. ("There's a New Helena now, but that's gone to pot.") She and her husband raised four children, who in turn have given her eight grandchildren and three great-grandchildren.

Her days now are filled with looking after the expansive vegetable garden and wondering what to do with what seems to be a bumper crop of apples ripening on the trees around her house.

Mattilda Slavicek at her backyard weather station. "She does it for the same pay her husband received: gratis." (Photo by John Danicic Jr.)

Last week, the family slaughtered a couple of dozen chickens; Slavicek slit their throats as dexterously as she always has. "Took us all day, you know, because you have to sit and talk about everyone else's news."

Twice a week, she goes to the senior citizens center in Jordan to play 500, looking slightly askance at those tables where poker is being played, even if it's only for pennies. Then it's home to check the thermometers at 6 p.m., then settle in for the news and "Wheel of Fortune."

Actually, she does get some consideration for her daily duties. Because she supplies the Jordan Daily Independent with its daily temperature record, she gets a free subscription to the weekly.

And the weather, in a perverse way, also may be trying to compensate her. During one of last week's electrical storms, a bolt of lightning apparently struck the house because her television set was burned out when she came home.

"We've been trying to tell Mother that she should get rid of that old black-and-white TV and get a color one," Kipka said.

Slavicek smiled: "Now I guess maybe I'll have to."

The birthday triplets in uniform: (L. to R.) Klara Egan, Alma Carson and Hilda Clauson. (ARGUS LEADER photo by John Danicic Jr., reprinted by permission.)

Triple-birthday triplets

COLTON, S.D. — We all have our bench marks for remembering the years, whether the weather on the Fourth of July, a death in the family or a child that was born.

How often have you heard people refer to a year in terms of the hundred-year flood (1969) or when the powderhouse blew up (1936)?

Klara, Alma and Hilda have their own method. It's unique in its design and exclusive to them, for they're the only ones who remember whether it was the year of the blue-and-white striped sundress (1950) or the peach lace shift (1979).

This is the year of the red-and-white print for The Triplets, who for 31 years have celebrated their birthdays together and, since 1960, have celebrated in identical dresses. Right down to the pearl necklaces.

"We were ready to give it up, but Hilda said let's do it one more year," Klara Egan said of three who celebrated their 82nd birthdays this month. "Maybe next year."

Klara Egan, Alma Carson and Hilda Clauson are not triplets by birth, but by neighboring. The Carsons, you see, settled in rural Colton, while the Egans were just over the hill going down into the Skunk Creek Valley near here and the Clausons were up the road.

Neighbors were a bit more neighborly in those days, it seems, not distracted by a show on television or tennis club in Sioux Falls. Conversation was still considered a form of entertainment.

Such conversing led the three to discover in 1950 that they shared not only the same month of birth, but year of birth. Since then, they've celebrated together.

Ten years later, Mrs. Clauson got the bright idea that they should dress alike for that special day chosen from among the birthdates of the 3rd, 5th and 12th.

"We went to Dell Rapids and picked out blue-and-white striped sundresses," Mrs. Egan says, smiling with the memory. A photograph shows them out on the lawn, huge red corsages draped over their shoulders.

"It was a typical South Dakota July day. We had the party outside and it was so windy, we had to keep a lot of food on our plates."

There was blue paisley in 1968, a daisy print in 1969 and bright pink in 1973. Difficulty in finding three identical dresses was solved when a Colton woman, Mrs. Fred Mews, began sewing them.

For their 80th birthdays, though, they cut loose with store-bought again, selecting a delicate, peach-colored lace in which to greet the 200-some people who came to an open house.

The party was fitting tribute to three women who have learned the value of maintaining a friendship. Still having the chuckle, they remember the time they left their husbands home and went to Minneapolis for the weekend.

"We wanted to see Cinerama," Mrs. Egan said. "Stayed two nights. And the movie was 'Windjammer.' "

"Oh, you even remember that," Mrs. Clauson said. Things have changed since those first sundresses. Mrs. Carson is now widowed and the Egans have moved into town, while the Clausons are still on the farm. Hairstyles have changed and figures have shifted — "Yes, we're getting stomachs on us now," Mrs. Egan said.

This year's scrapbook photograph will show that, no doubt, and rightly so. It's a sense of history that shouldn't be girdled or sucked in.

Besides, these are women comfortable with each other, friends who understand. Neighbors who still talk to each other.

UPDATE: Klara Egan died in 1982. Alma Carson and Hilda Clauson still reside in Colton.

Painted late in John Banvard's life, this oil study gives some idea of the style of the largest painting in the world. No trace of the original mammoth painting remains. (Photo courtesy Robinson State Museum, Pierre, S.D.)

Long art and short life

When John Banvard fled to Watertown, S.D., it was to a death in genteel poverty, his millions squandered, his claim to fame cracked and faded.

Since 1891, his body has lain in Mt. Hope Cemetery, his gravestone the only remaining evidence of a man who perhaps was once the world's richest artist, creator of a painting that made him the toast of European society.

How this man and his painting — the world's largest — ended up in Watertown is a story of showmanship and artistry, castles and technology. Little remains, except a chuckle on the other end of a phone when an inquiry is made.

After a life of firsts, Banvard died "a totally obscure figure, and probably rightfully so," says John Hanners, a teacher at Allegheny College in Meadville, Penn., who wrote his doctoral

John Banvard. "He probably was the richest artist who lived until the time of Picasso; certainly the richest 19th century artist." (Photo courtesy Robinson State Museum, Pierre, S.D.)

dissertation on Banvard. "He advanced art for his time, but probably ended up behind the times."

Banvard gained fame and fortune by creating a 12-foot-high, 3-mile-long panorama depicting 1,200 miles of the Mississippi River, from the mouth of the Missouri to New Orleans. The painting was stored on huge cylinders that were unrolled to the accompaniment of a piano and narration by the artist.

The program, which took two hours, was the era's equivalent of the motion picture. Riverboats, forts and Indian settlements were shown in minute detail. As the years went by, Banvard updated the panorama. In 1862, he added a section showing Civil War scenes.

He made millions.

"The panorama was an easy thing to do," Hanners says. "All he needed was himself and a piano player. It was pure profit.

"He probably was the richest artist who lived until the time of Picasso; certainly the richest 19th century artist."

Banvard toured the capitals of Europe with his painting, and attracted huge audiences in America as well. He built a castle on Long Island. It seemed nothing could go wrong.

The artist was born in the early 1800s in New York City and received early training when he became scene painter for a theater operator. When the operator decided to avoid taxes through the innovative concept of floating his show down the river, Banvard, by default, became the first showboat scene painter.

Banvard later ventured out on his own, and spent 1841 to 1846 painting his "Panorama of the Mississippi." The painting became a success, due in no small part to Banvard himself.

"In his later years, he was, well, he was a showman, all right," Hanners says. Unfortunately, no amount of razzmatazz could offset his original error in painting his canvas with lead-based paint thinned with varnish instead of longer-lasting, high quality paint.

The continuous unrolling and rerolling no doubt cracked the paint, Hanners says, and, after about 30 years, there probably wasn't much left of it.

Nor was there much left of Banvard's millions. Never a good manager, he ended up in poverty, moving in 1879 to Watertown, where his son had settled. He died 12 years later.

No one is sure what happened to the painting.

It's known that part of it was cut up to serve as stage backdrops for Watertown's three opera houses. The gas lighting of the day was dim enough to disguise the damage, but the advent of electrical lighting eventually rendered it useless.

Stories abound, says Jerry Bowman, of the Watertown Regional Library. One tale is that the canvas was used as a drop cloth by a local paint company. Another says it was used as insulation material. Still another maintains that Banvard's grandchildren used the painting for scratch paper.

"I think it's lost to posterity," Bowman says.

Hanners, though, still harbors the hope that someone's memory simply needs to be jogged, that someone will come forward and say, "Heck, I've got 70 feet of that thing rolled up in my attic."

UPDATE: John Hanners reports that his interest in Banvard has developed into a full-time occupation. He had an article published in the April 1987 issue of *Minnesota History* magazine about Banvard and his painting and is currently writing a book on the subject.

"What..."

"If I'm gonna get hurt, I want a chance to make some money at it." (ARGUS LEADER photo by John Danicic Jr., reprinted by permission.)

Why cowboys cowboy

BROOKINGS, S.D. — There must have been a whiff of loco weed in the air the day a cowboy first tried his luck on a wild bronc.

The dare-you dollar bills thrown into somebody's hat wouldn't be reason enough; money didn't mean much to a man driving cattle between the Pecos and the Platte, where the only thing you could buy was time.

A pretty girl strolling by a cow town corral wouldn't be reason enough; women either tempted you off the range or gave you a reason to get back on it.

Respect? Well, that's closer, though there was no shame in declining to ride a 1 1/2-ton Brahma bull, no sneers to be met if a devil-eyed bronc flicked you off like a horsefly.

Ask a cowboy like Phil Swanson why he rodeos and he'll hem and haw, finally blurting that it's his life, whether a logical extension of ranching chores or a fascination that's failed to fade.

"It's the people, you know?" says the Canton, S.D., cowboy. "You could be flat broke and there'll always be a place to sleep and a meal to eat."

It's as good an explanation as any for a sport experiencing a rebirth in a country fallen Stetson-over-spurs in love with the West. Cowboy chic is the fashion, country music is the mood. It stands to reason, then, that rodeo is the entertainment.

That's why close to 300 cowboys and cowgirls have gathered this weekend to rodeo (it's a verb here, as is cowboying), including several men and women currently leading this year's standings of the International Rodeo Association.

The ghost riders — those wispy clouds backlit by a westering sun — were in the Friday evening sky as the opening ceremonies began with the Cowboy Prayer:

"Lord, we don't ask for any special favors, only that we may compete in this arena as in life's arena...living lives as pure as the wind that blows across the grass country of the West...so that when we reach heaven, you'll tell us our entry fees are paid."

A Statler Brothers recording of the National Anthem was played as a cowgirl paraded the American flag around the arena. Then a bareback bronc burst onto the rain-soaked sand, inciting a high-flying spirit that continued until the last bull deposited his rider on the same soil.

No one agrees on when or where rodeo began, though the best argument holds that Denver had its first in 1876. The Wild West shows turned corral roughhousing into an entertainment business and, in 1936, the Cowboy Turtles Association — "It took us a long time to get started, but we finally stuck our necks out" — was founded.

A professional group with professional ambitions, the cowboys went on strike until their demands for higher purses and added entrance fees were met. This group later became the Rodeo Cowboys Association, counterpart to the International Rodeo Association that sanctions this rodeo. No one goes on strike these days, though for the average entrant, the money usually is just enough to get to the next rodeo.

Swanson, for instance, is in need of some cash. About four months ago, the 19-year-old bull rider broke his pelvis in two places. Then, he was 12th in the world standings; now he figures he's down to 21st or 22nd. Friday night, he was deciding whether to chance a ride.

"I'll have to see how my bull bucks," he said, gazing down into the corral of horned muscle. "If he bucks good, I'll get on. I mean, I already know it's gonna hurt, so if I'm gonna hurt, I want a chance to make some money at it."

That logic may seem backwards until you understand that the rodeo animal is judged just as closely as the rodeo rider. A calm bull may give you an easy ride, but fewer points. A mean bull will wrench your muscles, but produce a higher score.

Swanson, who turned professional upon high school graduation, decided not to ride Friday night, but not for lack of courage. He overcame that a few weeks ago when he boarded a bull just to get that thought out of his mind.

"I was never so scared in all my life," he said, his teeth grinning with braces. "You think about (getting hurt) every time you get on, but the longer you wait, the worse it gets."

Dennis Peterson also sat out the rodeo, recuperating from a punctured lung, several broken ribs and a broken collarbone he got while riding Midnight Hank, a bull also in attendance this weekend.

"If you stay on top of 'em, you're not gonna get stepped on," he said in explanation of his accident. "I'd ridden him four times before, but this time..."

Peterson, who works at the Coast-to-Coast Store here, doesn't count on making a living from rodeo: "If you want to go hard and heavy, sure, you can make a good living. But the economy the way it is, and you see what happens when you get hurt, well, I can't see quittin' Coast-to-Coast to go cowboying."

Neither can he see quitting cowboying.

The reasons have changed a bit since those early days on the range. A hatful of dollars is taken seriously, if only to get you to the next rodeo. Showing off doesn't carry as much weight, since the cowboy boots in both halves of the outhouse are scuffed.

Respect? Well, that's still there, although the audience probably felt more sympathetic for those many riders who found their way onto the rain-soaked sand.

Gone — but not forgotten

SHERMAN, S.D. — Abandonment could not have been an unexpected fate for these people.

Having challenged adversity simply by coming out here, these pioneers likely accepted death as adversity striking a retaliatory blow. They understood, perhaps even preferred, that their descendents would concentrate on besting the land instead of tending their graves.

Thus, 10 cemeteries — out of 61 in Minnehaha County — have been left to wither under the harsh eye of the sun, the markers to topple against the strong arm of the wind. Family names have been ground away by blown sand; goldenrod has risen to obscure a sculpted Bible.

Some ghosts, of course, might be appalled by their descendents' neglect. Certainly, the broad expanse within four quartzite cornerposts southwest of here is evidence of once-lofty intentions. They obviously had expected to do well here, to have set aside such a large plot of land.

Now, however, the few gravestones are scattered and askew, adorned with beer cans and wild roses.

What happened?

"The more immediate things, those are the more important things, I guess," says Ray Novak, chairman of the newly formed Abandoned Cemetery Association of Minnehaha County.

Funded with $1,000 this year and achieving corporation status, the association has set out to reclaim these acres of rest, and has found a sideline in reuniting families and completing genealogies.

The project got its start when Novak and the late Elton Bissell founded the county genealogical society. Since no death records were kept here prior to 1908, and the only other records being what was assembled by the Works Progress Administration, they decided to delve into the tumble-down cemeteries for their answers.

What they found was places like the Taopi Cemetery near Colton, S.D., with its six graves. At first, they seemed a forgot-

Cemetery at Sherman, S.D. "Evidence of once-lofty intentions." (Photo by John Danicic Jr.)

ten half-dozen. Novak thought there were no relatives in the area anymore, figuring the Depression drove them west where work was rumored to exist — or at least into the mountains where the dust didn't blow so bad.

Now, he's got a line on a possible descendent of Archibald Bell, a Civil War veteran.

The same thing happened in Sherman, where relatives live nearby, but have long fallen out of the habit of tending some great-great-grandrelation's grave. Besides, there's something eerie about placing fresh flowers in the midst of a patch overgrown with thistles and littered with a rusty hay rake.

Then there's the history behind the tiny cemetery near Lyons. It was established by the Women's Christian Temperance Union; only tee-totalers were eligible to buy a plot.

It's little wonder that these final resting places have been abandoned. We tend to be uncomfortable about death, though we have been taught to respect the dead.

Perhaps there is a poetic justice in the cemeteries' fate. Nature, it seems, finally got the last laugh over the supposed conquerors of the soil. Unfortunately, nature isn't the only culprit in the deterioration.

Beer bottles tell the tales of parties, and toppled gravestones are evidence of mindless vandalism. Enforcement against such destruction is difficult since ownership of these cemeteries is a matter of confusion.

"It's a ticklish deal," Novak says. "Most of it is churches or other groups who think they own it, but really, only the individual lot owners have the property. The rest, nobody owns."

The association is using its status as a corporation to incorporate the cemeteries. It's spent $300 in Taopi, $400 in Sherman and has earmarked $50 for Burke, all to remount the gravestones and clear the brush.

When their allotted $1,000 runs out, "we'll wait 'til next year," Novak says.

UPDATE: Ray Novack and other members of the Minnehaha County Abandoned Cemetery Committee are still working hard to preserve the burial sites and markers from vandalism and neglect. The budget allocated to them is still $1,000 a year.

Majesty of simple things

BROOKINGS, S.D. — Like a stallion just broken, a Harvey Dunn painting demands a slow and careful approach.

It is most comfortable when you keep your distance, but will allow close inspection if you insist.

Only then, after you satisfy yourself by exercising the privilege of intimacy, do you realize there is a quality here that resisted the whip, a wildness that demands your distance, a demand you find yourself respecting.

It is in this untamed quality, saddled beneath a surface of thick paint, that the true beauty lies.

Harvey Dunn — there is a school in Sioux Falls named after him...and wasn't he the guy who painted that picture of that pioneer lady picking flowers on the prairie?

Yeah, that's the guy.

Unfortunately, there are a lot of people who know little more than that about the South Dakotan who was eulogized by Norman Rockwell and has been called one of the greatest illustrators of his time.

I had to include myself among that lot until last week when I visited the exhibit of Dunn paintings at the Memorial Art Center at South Dakota State University. Now I number myself among his many admirers.

Dunn's paintings of the Dakota prairie are the pictures we see in our minds and, like our visions, they look a bit muddled. The rusty colorations of "Injuns" only suggest the isolation of the two figures rolling across the grasses in an open wagon. The white blur of "30 Degrees Below" conjures a memory of a particular winter that was so bad.

They are startling pictures with their cerulean-and-salmon skies, their bright blue shadows adding depth to a golden slope of grassland. He was an artist of the bold stroke, often using a palette knife to build depth into a plowed field. Colors that jar when viewed up close dissolve into reality when given some space in which to breathe.

His people are strong figures with broad shoulders. Dunn's sensitive use of back-lighting to illuminate his subjects often results in their faces being nothing more than a suggestion, allowing the viewer to choose the emotion.

His sense of wind is as natural as an afterthought, whether conveyed in the laid-back ears of a ranch dog or the swirl of an apron above a muslin skirt.

Dunn, who died of cancer in 1952, characteristically would brush off such praise. Born near Manchester, S.D., in a house built next to an old buffalo path, Dunn always retained his sense of home even though he left the state in 1902, never to live here again.

The son of a homesteader, he honed his instincts at the Chicago Institute of Art, then applied to study in Delaware with Howard Pyle, America's foremost illustrator at that time.

In an excellent biography by Robert F. Karolevitz, who lives near Mission Hill, S.D., Dunn recalled that time: "All that I am really doing is carrying on the Howard Pyle idea...Howard Pyle did not teach art. Art cannot be taught. He did, however, lay constant stress upon the proper relationship of things...His main purpose was to quicken our souls that we might render service to the majesty of simple things."

Although immediately finding success as an illustrator, Dunn found himself caught up in the patriotism of World War I and volunteered to be one of eight official artists in Europe. His work was acclaimed as some of the most emotional to come out of the war.

Some of those illustrations at the museum in Brookings show us a different Dunn, mostly because they are detailed and do not exhibit the subtlety of shadow and light.

One reason for that is the very nature of an illustration, said Sheila Agee, an assistant to the curator. Illustrations are more stark because the artist must keep the reproduction quality in mind, she said. Thus, there is a garish quality to some of the pictures, a quality no doubt enhanced by the drama of the subject matter.

"Harvey Dunn in his studio." South Dakota Memorial Art Center Collection, Brookings, S.D. (Photo used by permission.)

Upon his return from the war, Dunn and his wife, Tulla, set up a studio in Tenafly, N.J., where he continued his career as illustrator. In 1939, a long association with *The Saturday Evening Post* ended when Dunn refused to alter an illustration of an ice harvest because he feared the effect would be ruined.

Of more importance to Dunn, however, was his role as a teacher. A typical class session, according to Karolevitz, was a walking lecture with numerous "Dunnisms" dropped throughout the evening.

A sampling: "A second thought is always dangerous." "An idea is not something you 'cook up.' It comes to you when your consciousness is open and receptive." "Beauty goes right along with conviction." "Without strength there is no tenderness."

In his younger days, he might have been described as a workaholic because of his prolific and punctual production. As he passed 40, however, the memory of the Dakota prairie began to work on him and he began returning to the state for the summer, a practice he kept up for the next 25 years. He rarely painted here, but made voluminous sketches that he later committed to canvas.

Depicted in those paintings that, in 1950, he presented to South Dakota State University are the drama of a prairie funeral in "I Am the Resurrection and the Life," the windswept innocence of "After School," and the independent stride in "A Driver of Oxen."

In 1970, the Memorial Art Center was built to better display the works of this most-Dakotan of prairie artists. Included in the display is the massive easel before which the strapping, 6-foot-1 Dunn painted. Upon that easel is a painting called "Homesteader's Wife."

I wish I could describe it to you, but it can only be felt. Again bathing his background in a blur of slate grays and blues, Dunn provoked a foggy image from which one of his strong young women emerges, tugging at the cow whose milk quenches the dusty prairie.

It is a dream-like picture except for her face. Beneath a haze of top-knotted hair, Dunn paints a face whose tired eyes have seen everything, but on this day see nothing. Yet the impression conveyed is that there is nowhere else this woman would rather be. It is her homestead, too, and her cow and her prairie.

And she is Harvey Dunn's, and he is ours.

"Where..."

Middle-of-the-road story

It has been lied about, chipped at, honored by, crashed into and haggled over in the course of its 140 years.

But the tri-state marker that has stood at the intersection of Iowa, Minnesota and South Dakota for all that time, stands no more.

And until something is done about it, the three counties surrounding the historical spot are breaking the law.

The catch is this: although the federal government owns the marker and enforces the fines levied for destroying an historical site, it won't provide any money to replace the iron post, destroyed last month when apparently hit by a truck.

"It HAS to be replaced. It's illegal not to have it there," says a perplexed Carol Mashek, president of the Minnehaha County Historical Society.

"There's no way to beat the federal government. But we're not getting any money, either."

Right now, the historical societies of Rock County in Minnesota, Lyon County in Iowa, and Minnehaha County in South Dakota are hanging fire on a decision by the National Registry to accept the monument on their register, thereby freeing federal funds.

If the bucks aren't forthcoming, then the societies have to go before budget-conscious county commissions, and if that fails, try to get a bill through Congress.

The marker, a 5-foot iron post erected smack-dab in the middle of the road, has stood at the intersection just north of Larchwood, Iowa, for 140 years.

Actually, it wasn't put in the middle of the road at the time—more like in the middle of some tall prairie grass, but surveyors will be surveyors and a road eventually was constructed, going around the post like a stream around a lonesome boulder.

Mystery has dogged the post for years with few knowing exactly who put it there in the first place.

IOWA
TRI-STATE
MARKER

Popular folklore credits Jefferson Davis, who went on to become president of the Southern Confederacy, with placing the marker during a surveying mission in 1859.

A 1913 article in the Sioux Falls Journal reported that "every early settler was interrogated. Indians were questioned and no possible clue was left unexplored," in tracing its history with all clues pointing to Davis.

Mrs. Mashek groans when she hears that story.

"Jefferson Davis was serving in the U.S. Senate in 1859, not traveling around with some survey team," she says. "That story got started by one of his relatives who lived around here."

The truth, she says, is that the marker was placed by Moses K. Armstrong who surveyed the western boundary of Minnesota back in 1859.

"The Jeff Davis story just ran rampant in the 1930s. A lot of people still believe it."

Regardless of who put it there, the post isn't there now. Instead, the chunks of iron and cement are stored in Rock Rapids, Iowa, where the Lyon County Sheriff is investigating who knocked it over.

The marker was rededicated in 1938 after the Minnehaha County Historical Society took steps to repair the crumbling post, chipped away by passing vehicles and souvenir seekers.

It was, as they say, a gala event with a crowd of 3,000 on hand plus four bands and a number of state and local dignitaries.

That heyday faded with the years, however, with curses resounding from some local residents who use the road daily and see the protruding post as a traffic hazard.

Those days of braking and swerving may not be over yet for federal law says a monument must be replaced on the exact spot.

Exactly.

Mrs. Mashek wants to see a bronze marker installed flush with the roadway to meet that requirement and erect another iron post to the side of the road.

The Tri-State Marker in its new location. Who put it there in the first place? (Photo by John Danicic Jr.)

Hundreds of photos like this were taken when the marker was in its original site. Each man is standing in a different state: (L. to R.) R.A. Rector, Andrew J. Berdahl, and C.A. Smith, all early residents of the area. The photo was taken during a rededication ceremony in 1938. (Photo courtesy Leonard Tripp.)

But Minnehaha County is just one-third of the voice that speaks for the monument. Rock County historians favor re-erecting the post as it was. The Lyon County chapter goes along with the bronze plaque.

Any disagreement is moot, however, since any sort of replacement requires money—a scarce commodity among many historical projects, Mrs. Mashek says.

That's why they're hoping the National Registry comes through with the money.

They may need it for bail.

UPDATE: The tri-state marker now stands out of harm's way at the side of the road, some distance from the actual junction of the three states.

A darned interesting dig

MITCHELL, S.D. — The walls of the trench are sharp with broken buffalo bones. Heat rises in shimmers from the crisp grass, blurring a distant grove of trees and intensifying the keen smell of creosote from the old railroad ties that mark a path through the rolling acre.

The rustle of a lake breeze through the cottonwoods gradually dissolves into the voice of Linda Ronstadt singing that she's tried and she's tried, but she can't say good-bye.

Four students, pink from the sun but beginning to tan, crouch over precise squares of black earth, brushing it by centimeters into dustpans. A pair of U.S. government-surplus bone cutters lie nearby, next to a serrated grapefruit knife.

What these four summertime archeologists find may rewrite all existing literature dealing with construction of Middle Missouri houses, destroying the theory that the early Mandan lived in earth dwellings.

Big deal, some of you say, yawning.

"People say, 'Why do you even worry about an archeological site?'" Darrel Fulmer says, repeating the tiresome question. "I'd like to say, 'Well, because it's darned interesting,' but that doesn't seem to cut mustard."

For the record, the Mitchell Prehistoric Indian Village is darned interesting. Located on a small promontory above Lake Mitchell, the village is thought to have been inhabited about 900 years ago in the year 1064 A.D., give or take 16 years.

It appears that the villagers lived in large lodges substantially constructed from a framework of posts covered with willow mats and grass thatch. The walls may have been plastered with mud and the walls of some seem to have been backed with earth.

A great amount of timber was used in these homes and they had to be reconstructed about every 12 years. Fulmer estimates that the village, in which the population is thought to have ranged from 700 to 1,400 people, was occupied for about 32 years, requiring at least two remodelings.

In addition, a fortification wall was erected around three sides of the camp. That also had to be replaced as the camp expanded.

Thus, the most likely reason for the camp's abandonment was that its timber supply became depleted since the villagers allowed no regrowth, preferring to keep the cleared areas open for farming.

Of course, that's just a theory — one of the many mysteries held by the grassy knoll gently pocketed with depressions that mark ancient home sites. Part of the settlement probably has been eroded by the lappings of Lake Mitchell, formed when Firesteel Creek was dammed in 1928.

The village first was mapped in 1922, then the Works Progress Administration excavated some burial mounds and a home site in 1938. The next excavation wasn't attempted until 1971 and Fulmer has been working as project director at the site for the past two years.

He estimates it will be another eight to 10 years before they can draw solid conclusions as to what life was like on the shores of Firesteel Creek in the 11th century.

"About every time we open up a new square, there's something we didn't expect," Fulmer says. Tanned and lanky, with a beard that grows in uneven lengths around his long face, Fulmer speaks with a quiet intensity; at times, he shyly apologizes when he fears he's becoming too detailed in his explanation.

"All my answers are convoluted," he admits. His smile comes easily.

To put it most simply, the Mitchell villagers were ancestors of the Mandan, the tribe first encountered by Europeans living in what is now North Dakota. They probably migrated to the Mitchell area from Iowa and Minnesota after a climate change in 900 A.D. brought warm, moist Gulf air into the northwest, favoring crop growth.

They built a village fortified by a 12-foot-wide ditch and a wall of timbers to protect them from the hunters already roaming the area. It must have been a confrontation.

Other parts have been destroyed by what Fulmer facetiously calls "unsystematic digging," better known as "Dad and the kids go hunting for arrowheads." Walking by one spot of scarred earth labeled as a collector's excavation, Fulmer shakes his head: "It's like a strip mine."

Fortunately, the area has been designated a National Historic Landmark and carries a $1,000 fine for anyone removing objects.

To better understand why taking a little half-inch piece of pottery carries such a toll, Fulmer explains how archeology works.

He starts with the theory that these people lived in a matriarchal society in which the mother is the head of the family and kinship is traced through her instead of the father. In such a society, each woman had the right to a specific design on her pottery. By checking the distribution of decorated pottery fragments throughout the site, Fulmer can connect a family group to a certain lodge.

If such fragments are removed or scattered throughout the site, theories cannot be proved nor disproved. History is lost, ending up in what he calls the proverbial cigar box of arrowheads.

"We build these houses of cards, but it's because we have no other evidence. When we're digging, we're also destroying that part of the site, so the idea is to destroy as carefully as possible so we can reconstruct it on paper."

Such reconstruction is being done by students from across the United States working on the site for college credit. They work with brushes, trowels and dustpans, gathering and sifting, sluicing and speculating.

"Is this anything more than wishful thinking?" Robin Primoff asks, holding up a small, pebble-like object.

"That," Fulmer replies, turning it over in his hand, "is a fragment of your imagination." Archeology, it seems, is the science of subtle differences. The spot where a post once stood, for example, is discovered by spotting a small circle of oh-so-slightly darker and finer soil. Determining whether something is a potsherd or a rock chip is an acquired talent.

"This place is lousy with pottery," Fulmer says, jumping down into a trench seemingly sprouting with fired clay chips along with bison femurs, dog jawbones and clam shells.

Everything found is taken to the laboratory at Dakota Wesleyan University in Mitchell and catalogued. Literally tens of thousands of pieces are stored in paper sacks and cardboard boxes stacked in closets. It is here that the shards of pottery are jig-sawed together, most often by Mrs. Fulmer.

Constantly having to remind himself that archeology is a patient science, Fulmer knows he must find as much as he can at this particular excavation before the summer ends because the project outline requires that his attention move to the lakeshore side of the site.

The site is open to visitors from 8 a.m. to 8 p.m. every day through Aug. 22. There is a small admission charge because the project is largely dependent upon donations. For that, you get a guided tour of the site, a chance to see how an archeologist works and a 15-minute videotaped explanation of the ancient village.

Try to imagine, the tape says, how future archeologists will interpret how we lived when they find our remains — how a slight depression on a stairstep will tell how much it was used, when and by whom.

It's darned interesting.

UPDATE: The site at Mitchell continues to come under scientific scrutiny, most recently by a group from the archeology lab of Augustana College in Sioux Falls, S.D.

The word trade center

BUFFALO TRADING POST, S.D.—Brandishing what looks like a small machete, Judson Foster whacks off a pepper-studded slab of German salami and another of mild Colby cheese.

If you want, he smears the two slices of white bread with mayonnaise before stacking it all together, wraps it in a sheet of wax paper and, for 80 cents, presents you with a sandwich you literally can sink your teeth into.

Washed down with a bottle of pop, it's the meal-of-the-day, everyday, at Buffalo Trading Post, a community of one building seven miles west of Colton, S.D. (north and west of Sioux Falls).

New faces stop conversation here, but they're welcomed, especially during hunting season when Foster says you can hardly get inside the white-board building.

"We get lots of lake trade here," says Foster, whose father, Donald, founded the trading post in 1927 as a farmers' market that thrived in the money-scarce years of the Depression.

Buffalo Trading Post is a sort of neighborhood grocery out in the middle.."of nowhere?"Foster suggests knowingly. No, more like the middle of somewhere, given the steady stream of customers who crunch across the gravel out front.

"Dad got this started as a place farmers could bring the eggs, cream, hides. We still buy eggs, but there's not as many farmers around as there used to be. Lot more acreage owners."

The post itself was moved out from the Colton lumberyard and a grocery store also moved down from now-extinct Shady Lane, a mile north and a mile west.

Today the grocery store is boarded up, and the trading post is doing all its business within earshot of a hay stacker's grinding hum in the neighboring field.

Foster, 39, has worked here since he was 19, moving back from a job in Sioux Falls after his father had a stroke. His eyes disappear in a grin for each customer. He enjoys the people he meets, the easy give-and-take of neighborly conversation.

"During harvest, all the farmers meet here in the morning to decide who'll do what. We're open all the time, too, it seems. Seven days, seven nights. It's a lot of hours."

Foster, at ease with his shirttails hanging out over a football player's build, pushes a broom across the hardwood floor softened by the shuffle of leather boots and the occasional paws of a dog. It's a crazy conglomeration of furniture he sweeps around—a few old car seats, two school desks, an easy chair.

As your eyes adjust from the bright sunlight to the shadowy interior, you see a great chestnut-colored dog lazing in the corner. He awakens to show you gleaming golden eyes and a demeanor that you don't want to mess around with.

He's a Chesapeake, both him and his father," Foster says. "I can't understand it. They can be the friendliest dogs during the day, but I leave them in here at night and the first sound they hear outside, they'll jump and bark, hit the door."

No wonder Forster never has had a problem with break-ins, despite the pennies—there must be thousands—he has stowed away in jars on the top shelf.

He pulls a half-empty pop bottle from the cooler that doubles as a sales counter. He'll close up a little early tonight, he tells customers. Has to go down to Sioux Falls.

But next morning, he'll be open for the farmer who wants to compare crop conditions, the house-wife who needs a quart of milk, the guy with a few stories to swap.

They still do a lot of trading up here, you see; it's just of a little different kind.

UPDATE: Judson Foster left the trading post in 1983, but the store is still open under new management.

(Photo by John Danicic Jr.)

FALL

"When..."

Autumn reverie

It's time again for long thoughts and slow looks, for taking more time than usual to consider ordinary things.

Autumn, more than the other seasons, seems to inspire reverie. Maybe it's the intangible aura of age washing over a countryside that barely a month ago was growing green. Maybe it's the prospect of a prairie winter and its ability to herd us indoors that makes these last moments in a brisk environment so appealing.

Or maybe it's the sky, especially fickle this time of year. One day, it hangs like a shroud, as softly gray as the underside of a dove; the next, it hovers with the brilliance of a jaybird's wing. The sun seems less harsh, no longer fading the blue expanse like a curtain left too long on a window. It sets fat and heavy, sinking through the haze of harvest earlier and with more finality than we'd like.

The changeability makes us think about our own changes. So we tend to dawdle, lazing in bed a few minutes more, taking the side streets across town instead of breezing down main drags.

What was a summer stroll now turns into an autumn shuffle. Dusty shoes betray those who wander to the sidewalk's edge where leaves lie brushed aside like shards of carnival glass. Trees begin to poke sharply at the sky and hedges turn traitor to their appointed task of providing privacy.

In the country, the cornfields are beginning to shudder in the breeze; what once was a smooth whisper now is sharpened to a raspy wheeze. The stalks seem more fragile, standing like tired soldiers of the summer prepared to surrender.

Swirls of birds swoop from field to field, scalloping the sky with their bobbing flight. They settle with a cackle on the ripening corn, only to soar again at the intrusion of a curious farm dog.

The smell of woodsmoke begins to hang in the air, and the whine of a buzzsaw carries less the thought of another dead elm than the prospect of warming fires. Neighbors start to compare the merits of ash and birch, all the while seeking a lead on where they can get some ash and birch.

We start to think of pumpkin pie, one of the truly seasonal dishes that never should be made before Oct. 1, nor served after Jan. 31. Apple cider finds its way into our refrigerators and acorn squash becomes autumn's zucchini.

We forget that we'd tired of oatmeal and remember the comfort of marshmallows — the little ones — floating in a cup of cocoa after a football game.

Yet all is not as languorous as it seems. There is an underlying momentum, a scurrying among the squirrels as they skitter around treetrunks, chasing each other as if pursuing their own shadows. There are things to be done in the crisp autumn air, screens to be stored and plants to be brought in, cars to be waxed and carrots to be pulled.

It is as if we are tucking ourselves in for the duration, pulling our memories of warm days at the lake around our minds like a woven afghan. We realize this may be the last chance to let our thoughts wander before finding ourselves preoccupied with keeping warm, shoveling out and starting up.

And so we meander through autumn, recalling tasks left undone, tasks accomplished, wondering at the grasp of squirrels and second-guessing the first hard frost.

It is a good time of the year, a harvest that goes beyond the realm of the fields.

"Who..."

A common man, an uncommon tenacity

VALLEY SPRINGS, S.D. — Peder Phillips won't end up in the history books, and more's the pity.

Those volumes seem reserved for heroes, villains and influential people and Phillips, by his own admission, is a common man.

His contribution to society is nothing more crucial than recollecting a hailstorm on Aug. 13, 1914, so severe that it cut the horses' hides as they huddled in the pasture.

Then there was Dec. 13, 1938, which was "raw and inclined to be a little snowy." He towed logs most of that day.

Or Feb. 14 of this year, when "the early dawning in Kaleidoscope colors caused a sparse snow near the house to become pinkish from reflection."

That's worth remembering.

It's all down on paper, 68 years of the stuff that makes up our common lives. Chores, weddings, the death of a horse — Phillips has recorded them in prose sometimes terse, sometimes sentimental.

"I call it the story of a common man," he says, looking over the 25 bound volumes that grew out of a youngster's diary. "You can get all sorts of books about professional people — doctors, lawyers, politicians. But what do we care about politicians? They got their problems and we got ours."

Phillips speaks with sureness in a voice that betrays his Norwegian ancestry. At 87, he still does fieldwork, though his sturdy, ham-handed frame is beginning to sag like the walls of his wind-scoured barn. His lips are chapped by years of Dakota weather. He, like his farm southwest of Valley Springs, is aging.

This reader of Thoreau and Emerson is not content to wither away, though, without leaving his mark upon the world. Call it a smudge; common men aren't inclined to be flashy.

Phillips' story is a treasure to those who will recognize it as such. He already knows that history is told in terms of mountains and valleys; the plateaus rarely get credit. But much of a common man's life is spent on a plateau, chopping wood, visiting relatives, going to funerals, pausing for a sunset.

"This is what bugs me," he says, straightening in his chair. "So many people don't see these simple things."

Aug. 24, 1964: "...I accompanied the trucker to the pasture and directed him to where Broncho had died. Gives a fellow a sad feeling to see a faithful horse trucked away in death."

May 13, 1924: "Rain, sleet and snow. Bad day. It seemed unreasonable to see farmers planting corn with snow scooting around them. Bu-r-r-h!"

There are entries in which he recalls the sweat coursing down his body on a strenuous day or going to see "The Stand at the Apache River" at the old Egyptian Theater in Sioux Falls. Over years of birdwatching, he's seen the flyways change.

The value of these recollections?

You've just experienced it, for how long would the Egyptian Theater remain in our memory if it wasn't jogged once in a while? And remember the year Canada geese flew over Rowena? Phillips' fascination with birds has colored much of his writing. This summer's mild weather brought many southern birds farther north and his sighting of a scarlet tanager — unusual for this region — was occasion for a soft chuckle.

"Seeing that tanager did more for me than drinking a gallon of whiskey."

It was the weather that provoked his first entry.

On Feb. 17, 1913, the weather warmed so much so that Phillips' brother, Ben, got antsy and decided to get a head start on discing the cornstalks. It was an event worthy of note and Phillips hasn't quit noting since.

Each entry begins with a description of the weather. A High Plains farmer grows up with one eye on the sky and what's

---

Peder Phillips and his journal. "So many people don't see these simple things." (ARGUS LEADER photo by John Danicic Jr., reprinted by permission. »

VOL. I.
VOL. II.
RECORD
7/12/'18.
10/15/'22-
300
VOL. III.
RECORD
9/30/'25
500
VOL. IV.
VOL. V.
4/29/'29-5/16/'32
S 300
R
500
VOL. VI.
5/17/'32-8/25/'35
S 304
R
500
VOL. VII.
8/26/'35-
1/17/'39
S 304
R
500
400

VOL. IX 9/18/'42 6/18/'46
VOL. X. 6/9/'46 12/17/'48
VOL. XI. 12/18/'48 2/26/'51
VOL. XII 2/27/'51 5/24/'53
VOL. XVI 5/17/'60 10/5/'62

up there usually supercedes all other events of the day. Consider the entry of Sept. 11, 1930:

"Foggy this morning. A very fine day. Nice and warm with south winds." Only later, do we discover it's his wedding day.

His and Florence's, that is. Phillips corrected an earlier error some time ago by including both names: "I used to write 'we,' but now I say 'Florence.' Years from now, nobody'd know who 'we' is."

His technique is simple: He carries small notebooks — the kind you get from seed corn companies — into which he jots thoughts during the day. The next morning, upon his 5:30 rising, he transcribes the previous day's note into a large volume.

He worries that something gets lost in the translation.

"The first time you write it down, the idea is going just ahead of your pencil, but when you repeat it in the book, sometimes the words get turned around. You get ambiguous, you know what I mean?"

He's been tempted several times not to make his daily record. One time, he was seasick during his return from World War I, but he kept it in his head until able to write. The hard times also were hard to put down on paper.

"To tell the truth, it takes a lot of gumption to keep it up, but you start letting it go and you kill the idea of it."

Now that he's kept it up all these years, he's wondering what to do with it. Several people have contacted him about making it into one book, but he thinks it means more if it remains in his handwriting. The Center for Western Studies at Augustana College also has expressed an interest.

"The only thing I worry about here is fire," Phillips says, "but if I put them up in Augustana College, I can't go see them like I do now. It's a fuss knowing what to do."

Originally published 11-1-81 as "The story of a common man — 68 years worth."

UPDATE: Peder Phillips is still writing in his diaries.

"What..."

An oasis of tolerance

MINNEAPOLIS, Minn. — Summer takes its leave with a withering glance. The last tomatoes dangle from barren stakes like forgotten ornaments. Even chrysanthemums, hearty dawdlers among flowers, seem more pale with each frost. Those who take pleasure from the soil could not be begrudged a sigh of regret.

Yet perhaps more than those who follow any other avocation, gardeners appreciate the cycles of nature. Already, David Moehnke of Burnsville haunts his mailbox for seed catalogs. E.C. Culbert has put up enough vegetables from his Portland Av. garden to last most of the winter.

They, and the other 130 or so members of the Men's Garden Club of Minneapolis, are marking the new season, just as the club has marked the years since it was founded in 1943. The group is what the name implies: The only members are men who like to garden.

In a world where the idea of a men's club still evokes images of clattering poker chips, the roar of a touchdown scored or the *splitch* of a beer being popped, the garden club is a sort of wholesome boy's night out. They meet in a church basement. The choices of drinks with the evening meal are milk, water or coffee.

It all begins to sound like a gathering of pansies, and that's not a true picture. Yet for a man who has felt the sidelong gazes of those who perceive gardening as something less than a macho pursuit, the club is an oasis of tolerance.

"I'm a novice gardener and there's so much I can benefit from here without feeling intimidated," says Rich Bonlender, the newest member and, at 29, one of the youngest. He is garden project manager of the Self-Reliance Center, which rents plots to urban farmers accursed with postage-stamp yards.

"Admittedly, I first thought gardening was rather hokey, but as I got more involved in the community gardening thing, I just got caught up in the enthusiasm people had for their gardens. Now I've got two plots and I watch them like they were little babies. The other day, someone stole a couple of tomatoes and an eggplant and it was like a loss in the family."

A similar emotion brought Neal Whitfield of Minnetonka into the club when he moved here three years ago.

"I always liked gardening, but I never had the time, being a farmer in Ontario," he says, a Canadian lilt softening his speech. He sighs. "I love the soil."

Neighbor and fellow member Howard Berg steps up: "Neal here, he plants everything I throw out." Whitfield smiles and shrugs: "I just can't let anything die."

There are about 130 members in the club, which meets the second Tuesday of each month from September through May at Lake Harriet United Methodist Church. You find them simply by following the steady hum swarming up the stairwell, punctuated at times with the rumbling bass of men's laughter. They gather for an evening meal catered by several women of the church. A scan of heads in the room reveals more skin than hair, but the conversation is as vigorous as a patch of weeds.

After the men clear the tables, the meeting begins. Verner Carlson of the Sunshine Committee, which keeps track of the members' well-being, reports on someone with "ticker trouble." Joseph Stenger, in charge of maintaining the club's Community Fragrance Garden at 19th St. and Aldrich Av. S., tells of doing some weeding duty when one of the several vagrants who sleep there looked up at the flowers and said, "Gee, it's too bad those aren't edible."

Again, a roll of appreciative laughter. A spirit of camaraderie cloaks these men like a sheet thrown over tomatoes to protect them from early frost. Berg joined four years ago out of love of gardening, "but it's the comradeship of the fellas that keeps me coming back."

The first men's garden club was formed in 1928 in Chicago by an engineer, Leo W. Nack, who discovered there were lots of men who were of the opinion that gardeners need not be attached to a club where the principal membership was of the opposite sex. Today, there are more than 170 affiliated clubs with 9,000 members across the country.

No women ever have tried to join the Minneapolis club, says historian William Hull, "but I don't think there'd be a problem if any did." As it stands now, women — "wives and sweethearts," according to the club newsletter, *The Garden Spray* — are invited to the annual auction, the Christmas party and one of two garden tours during the summer.

Nationally, men have a great impact on the gardening business, out-spending their female counterparts, according to Gardens for All, a national association. In 1984, men spent an average of $209 on garden materials, compared with $164 spent by women. In fact, the composite ideal gardener, the association says, is a 30- to 49-year-old, college-educated, business or professional man, married, with children, earning $40,000 a year or more and living in the suburbs of cities in the West.

Demographics may not carry much weight with Ed Culbert, who joined the club in 1945 and, at 86, is the oldest member. He joined because he ran a garden program at Lincoln Junior High School, where he was principal. Now he and his wife, Barbara, grow all the produce they need to take them through the winter.

"I was raised in gardening," he says. "My grandfather had a potato patch in Soudan, in the Vermillion Range. He was a miner by trade, but raised enough to get them through the winter. That's where I got my first gardening experience."

Experience is what appeals to Dave Moehnke, who is nurturing a yardful of perennials in Burnsville. He's an expansive man, in presence and in speech. Among the stolid tillers emeritus of the group, he seems like the eager child who can't believe his luck.

"What a wealth of information is here," he says. "Literally hundreds of years of knowledge between some of these guys. I'm a practicing rookie and it's kind of fun to throw out a problem and get 15 different ideas of how to solve it. The knowledge just pours out of some of these guys."

If you doubt, just ask him about his chrysanthemums. Huge things, he says, and all because he was advised to pinch back all the buds until the Fourth of July. Works on peonies, too, says Howard Berg.

Moehnke, a sales manager for a tobacco company, is on the road a lot, so gardening for him is a form of therapy. "I love to go home and literally get my knees dirty," he says. "I've got a teen-age son who thinks I'm insane because I like mowing the lawn."

Of course, membership is a double-edged trowel. As Dwight Stone said upon inducting Rick Bonlender into the club, "I trust you will find that almost to the man, members are willing to stop whatever they are doing and answer your questions. And we hope, in time, that we can call on you when we need to know what's eating (our) tomatoes."

Over the years, the Men's Garden Club has quietly spread its horticultural influence over the city. In addition to establishing the Fragrance Garden behind the Minneapolis Society for the Blind, the club has planted flowering crabapple trees and evergreens in Lyndale Park, and there is a flower and vegetable show each August.

The Men's Garden Club in America also adopted an official song at its 1984 convention. It isn't sung at the local meetings, but like those little thermal Gro-Cones, it's nice to know someone came up with it should the need ever arise. It's sung to the tune of "The Marines' Hymn" and goes like this:

All across our big fine nation
Men's Garden Clubs abound.
We try to help each other
Make the best use of our ground.
So be sure your friends know who we are
And what our clubs can do.
For in helping others on their way
Our greatest joy is found.

Originally published 10-9-85 as "Men's garden clubbers raise food, friendship."

"Where..."

Gold in them hills

CANTON, S.D. — The tales of gold seem, at first, to be creations of a poet's mind.

Of course there is gold in Newton Hills this time of year, great leaf-laden trees of it, every bough dripping with nature's wealth that happens to be the color of man's desire.

You can shuffle through it, roll in it, kick it and crumble it, but it never will be the stuff from which prime interest rates are set.

There is, however, much more than the poet's rich images in the slopes rising from the Big Sioux River bottom seven miles south of Canton, S.D.

Or so they say.

There's gold—and silver—in them thar hills. And state law prevents anyone from ever getting rich from what many dismiss as a legend.

The tale springs from the diary of Earl Boyce, an early settler who wrote of a large caravan of California miners forced off the prairie and into the hills early in June 1859.

The caravan supposedly carried gold and silver bullion for the federal government, according to research done by the state Game, Fish and Parks Department.

Pursued by a band of hostile Indians, renegades and horse thieves, the caravan joined with a group of friendly Snake Indians having a pow-wow in the densely wooded hills.

On June 4, the pursuers attacked and the battle lasted one moon, or about a month, Boyce wrote. A band of Sioux then attacked the entire lot and emerged victorious after two weeks of fighting.

All the miners were killed and buried with the Indians somewhere in the region that in 1947 became Newton Hills State Park.

The gold and silver bullion—no one knows how much—was buried with them.

It may all be a legend.

Carl Anderson, who convinced state officials the land should be set aside as a park, dismissed it with a chuckle. Many residents do the same and no comprehensive history of Lincoln County ever has been compiled, relegating any speculation to just that—speculation.

Then again, it may all be true.

But there is a state law—41:03:01:05 to be exact—prohibiting anyone from destroying, damaging or removing any historic relics on lands owned or leased by the parks department without written permission from the department secretary.

So the treasure will remain buried, but not so the wealth of history wound in and around the stands of bur oak that blanket the park.

Frank and Jesse James are said to have hidden there after their great bank robbery in Northfield, Minn., "borrowing" horses from several farmers in the area.

There also is an account of horse thieves who maintained a permanent camp there, living in dugouts still visible as hollow depressions in the park. But, cautions the state release, there is no concrete proof for any of these accounts. Even the word "historical" is enclosed by quotation marks on the cover letter.

None of that should deter visitors, however. Set aside in an effort to keep firewood gatherers from razing the territory, the park covers 820 acres—948 with the beach area of Lake Lakota southeast of the main grounds.

"I thought the people were, well, they were going to destroy the trees down there," said Anderson, a local attorney who led efforts to designate it as a park in the 1940s.

Many owned land in 40-acre tracts, strictly for firewood purposes. Anderson, a Canton resident since 1937, went to each and obtained options on the land for about $20,000, he estimated.

"Didn't make any money on it, either," he said, crediting his friendship with the residents for their willingness to sell. "I just wanted to see it turned over to the state."

He's not sure who the park was named after. Indeed, no one seems to know.

But deep within a tattered volume of South Dakota history, there is a short paragraph on Newton Hills, apparently the only published data about the park.

Newton Hills, it said, was named after William Newton who homesteaded there at an early date.

And that could be a legend, too.

"Why..."

The missing ingredient

It's autumn. The calendar said so and the trees agree. Here in the city, logic tells us that autumn is here.

Yet something is missing. A scent is absent.

Oh, there is the acrid smell of fresh asphalt, sign of the final flurry before winter. And there is the sour odor of rotting vegetables in the yards of families sated with zucchini bread.

But the season seems incomplete without that most autumnal of smells, a scent carried by great billows of smoke rising from scorched patches of ground, that slightly sweet, slightly damp scent of burning leaves.

They call it open burning now and there are laws against it. Across the state, cities and towns forbid the smirching of good Minnesota air. Here in the Twin Cities, a few exceptions are granted for burning along the rivers, if the fire department needs some practice or for the odd university bonfire. If you grew up in the urbs and burbs after the burning was banned, you might not miss what you never had.

But if you moved here from the rural regions, where the air quality is less rigorously monitored (you can tell each spring by the thawing feedlots and the anhydrous ammonia), you know something is missing.

A bonfire of autumn leaves is not so much the culmination of a task as the climax of ritual. Believe me. The yard of the farm where I grew up was about an acre's worth of elm, hackberry, locust and black walnut trees. It was too daunting to scan the expanse, so we simply began raking, focusing on the cluttered semicircle within our immediate vision. Progress was measured by the width of swaths, the popability of blisters and the number of wheelbarrow-loads trundled to the driveway.

All afternoon, the smoke rolled across the yard, permeating our clothes, obscuring our view. Our noses burned. Our eyes smarted. It was great!

One year, for what must have been a good reason at the time, we tossed all the leaves into the manure spreader, which Dad unloaded in the field across the road. They were dispersed in a matter of minutes. We smelled only of sweat. It was weird.

For one thing, such a strategy subverted the philosophy of task and reward. Whenever leaves were burned, the payoff was in s'mores, charred marshmallows squished between sooty graham crackers and half a Hershey bar. Exhausted after a day tramping the lawn, we still made a production of choosing the right roasting stick. The tip could not be so thick as to disembowel the raw marshmallow, nor so thin as to provide too little support during the roasting, inevitably leading to marshmallow suicide.

I could continue to rhapsodize at some length at the signs of autumn outside a city. There is the musty smell of corn drying and the eerie rustle of the stalks and the sight of soybeans shriveling to rattling skeletons, although even that's behind schedule this year, what with all the rain. The cawing of the crows rises a few decibels. You root for the ambitious squirrel struggling to get an entire ear of corn up a tree.

But I live in the city now, where squirrels stow filched garden produce and discarded Twinkies. The trees turn into all their best hues, but the leaves then are stuffed into green garbage bags that sit on curbs, as big and misshapen as those cucumbers that hid all summer beneath the vines.

So how can you tell that it's autumn in the city? There are ways.

Christmas decorations are one of the first signs, now back in a store's farthest corners but poised to spring to featured display after Halloween.

Crocuses are coming up where you planted them when you thought it was autumn but it was only an unseasonably early cold snap and now the unseasonably late heat wave has them all confused.

The workers on Hennepin Av. are wearing long sleeves in the mornings, while wind surfers on Lake Calhoun are starting to wear wet suits again.

"A bonfire of autumn leaves is not so much the culmination of a task as the climax of ritual." (Photo by John Danicic.)

Mothers are in the grocery stores with their college-age sons, trying to make sure the new apartment is stocked with enough green beans and corn to counteract the Doritos and Ho-Hos.

Store racks are plump with parkas and swimsuits in preparation for the first blizzard and its distant cousin, the Caribbean cruise.

Perhaps most obviously, the highways are filled with people driving out of the city to see the autumn colors. People who might light a campfire and have a wiener roast. Who might, when nobody's looking, throw on some leaves and take a few deep breaths.

And who might, if they're persistent, find a stick just right for marshmallows.

INDEX